Second printing . . . . . . April, 1967

Bob Pettit: The Drive Within Me
by Bob Pettit with Bob Wolff

© 1966 by Prentice-Hall, Inc., Englewood Cliffs, N.J.

Library of Congress Catalog Card Number: 66-14357

Printed in the United States of America

T 07848

PRENTICE-HALL INTERNATIONAL, INC., *London*
PRENTICE-HALL OF AUSTRALIA, PTY. LTD., *Sydney*
PRENTICE-HALL OF CANADA, LTD., *Toronto*
PRENTICE-HALL OF INDIA (PRIVATE) LTD., *New Delhi*
PRENTICE-HALL OF JAPAN, INC., *Tokyo*

To the St. Louis Hawks and The Game of Basketball.

The Publisher wishes to acknowledge the assistance of Pete Finney of the New Orleans States-Item who helped greatly in the early development of this book idea.

Contents

Chapter 1 ● ON THE BENCH ● "Attention, please. For St. Louis, Cliff Hagan in for Bob Pettit."

Baltimore's Civic Center was jammed to capacity and even with the crowd cheering wildly, I could hear the public address announcement ringing in my ears. I slapped Cliff on the back and wished him luck and headed for our bench.

It was the fourth quarter and we trailed by a couple of points in a game we had to win. Baltimore led, two games to one, and another defeat would eliminate us from the National Basketball Association playoffs.

I kept looking at the clock, watching the seconds tick off and each second brought the St. Louis Hawks closer to defeat and brought me closer to retirement. This was to be my last season of professional basketball and—if we lost—my last game.

I looked at coach Richie Guerin, sitting on the bench a couple of seats away from me. I was hoping to attract his attention . . . hoping he would send me back in . . . but his eyes were riveted on the game. The frustration welled up within me as the seconds continued to tick.

It was not right. This was the one thing I feared, the one thing I couldn't accept. I didn't want to end my career sitting on the bench. I didn't want to go out this way. I wanted to be out there playing right to the end . . . why couldn't Richie see that was the way it should be? Why didn't he send me back into the game?

Suddenly, I had a feeling of anger and I was directing it at

Richie Guerin and that was unfair. It wasn't Richie's fault. If I were in his place, I would do the same thing he was doing.

I had been injured three times during the season, the last injury being a torn ligament in my left knee. I had the knee in a cast for three weeks and when the cast came off shortly before the playoffs it left my leg so weak I was of little help to the team.

So, we came up to that fourth game and Richie called me into his office.

"Bob," he said, "I'd like to do something tonight, but I won't do it without your approval. I've seen you struggling out there and I'd like to start Cliff Hagan in your place. If he's hot, he will stay in, and I'll use you as a substitute. I think you'll be more effective coming off the bench."

I was disappointed because I always like to play in important games, but I had to agree with Guerin's decision.

"Richie," I said, "you're doing the right thing. I would do the same thing if I were you."

But I wasn't Richie Guerin. I was Bob Pettit and it was my career which was coming to an end . . . an inglorious end at that . . . and as the seconds kept ticking, the maddening urge to get back in became so intense it was all I could do to control myself.

It was almost over. I was coming to the end of an 11-year career in the NBA. I was the leading scorer in the history of the game, the first player to score more than 20,000 points. I had been the scoring champion twice and twice was named the Most Valuable Player in the league. I had scored more points in the playoffs than any other player, but none of that could help me now. All that was in the past. In the present there was only frustration. I was ending my basketball career just as I had started it.

It's funny how things go through your mind so quickly. As I watched the clock ticking, much of my youth raced wildly, yet vividly, through my thoughts.

I remembered my freshman year at Baton Rouge High School. I was a member of the junior varsity basketball team.

That is to say I was on the squad, but I could hardly consider myself a member of the team.

I was always the last player to go in the game. I would go in when we were far ahead or far behind and I would play maybe a minute or so and after the game the fellows would be getting showered and dressed and they would talk about the game and about the points they scored.

"How many did you get, Jim?" one of them would ask.

"Six," Jim would say.

"Four," another would say.

"I got eleven," somebody else would say proudly and I always tried to make believe I wasn't listening because I didn't want them to ask me how many points I scored. I didn't want them to ask because I didn't score a point all season . . . not one stinking point.

I remember we were scheduled for a road game. We were going to play in Zachary, Louisiana, about fifteen miles north of Baton Rouge and the team was going by bus and I went to school all excited because it was my first bus trip with a team. I was very proud of myself because it made me feel like a big, professional athlete.

When I got to school I learned the bus had broken down and the trip would be made by car, but they didn't have enough room so they had to leave some players home and I was one of them. I can still remember watching the car pull away with the team and me left standing there. I could have cried.

I went home that night and I lay in bed for a long time before I could sleep. I thought about being the star of the team and making that trip to Zachary and getting in the game and scoring maybe 16 or 18 points while the crowd roared.

The crowd cheered wildly in the Baltimore Civic Center. The Bullets had won. It was over . . . the game . . . the season . . . my career . . . everything.

So this is how you go out, I thought. Sitting on the bench in Baltimore, Maryland, watching the Hawks lose by six points and unable to do anything about it.

I picked up my warm-up jacket and walked slowly toward the dressing room thinking of the injustice of it all . . . feeling the frustration . . . torn by the desire to help and the pain of being unable to help . . . thinking how the end was really no different from the beginning.

Chapter 2 ● IN THE BEGINNING ● It began in Baton Rouge, Louisiana and the people of that city may never know the danger it faced on December 12, 1932. On that day, the telephone rang in the sheriff's office and the voice on the other end informed the sheriff he had become a father.

If anybody was thinking of knocking over the local bank that would have been the time. The sheriff was too excited to do anything about it. His wife had just given birth to a nine and one half pound boy, their first and only child. They called me Robert E. Lee Pettit, Jr.

I was big at birth and I figured to be a big man. My dad stood 6' 4" and my mother was 5' 8" and she had four brothers who ranged from 6' 2" to 6' 5".

I may have been born in the middle of the basketball season, but unlike other players who shot hook shots from their crib with a rattle, I was not born to play basketball.

Mom was from Mississippi. She attended Louisiana State University and settled in Baton Rouge. Dad was born in Denver, but spent many years near Baton Rouge in a community called The Plains where his mother's family had always lived. He was an adventurer in the John Wayne mold, except he actually did the things they make into movies. Few men, I believe, have lived a more exciting life than my father.

He went to high school in Denver, played basketball at Westminster College and joined the Army in 1917. He served 18 months in the artillery and saw action in Belgium and France.

At the time he was discharged, his uncle was Adjutant Gen-

eral of the State of Colorado and Dad signed on as a Colorado
State Ranger, which was more dangerous at the time than
World War I because there were more than 10,000 Colorado
miners striking and at war with the constabulary.

When my father reported for duty, the captain asked, "Where
do you want your body shipped?"

My father said he didn't care, just to roll it in a ditch somewhere. He stayed with the Rangers about five months, then
moved on. He had inherited some property in Baton Rouge and
decided to go there.

My father and his brother ran a dairy farm on their property
but Dad soon found the life too dull. He joined the sheriff's
office as a chief criminal deputy and that was more to his liking.
Dad served the parish for 16 years. He had met my mother and
married her in 1929, and in 1932, Dad was elected sheriff.

For the first four years of my life, my father wore the star
and he always kept the car with the siren in the driveway and
I would play with the siren.

There were always 20 or 30 loaded guns of all sizes around
the house, but out of my reach. I was seven when I got my
first gun and I guess that is when I became interested in hunting. It is one of my favorite pastimes, but I haven't had an
opportunity to do much hunting during the past 20 years
because the hunting season always conflicted with basketball.

My family was well off, but get it straight, I never was allowed
to loaf as a boy. I worked Saturday mornings for my uncle,
Walker Pettit, in the family's hardware store. I was paid fifteen
cents, which I spent immediately for the movies. They soon
raised my pay to a quarter.

I ran errands, swept the floor and sold fish hooks. I was the
king of the fish hooks. The job did one thing for me, it taught
me thrift.

After being sheriff, my father was Postmaster for nine years
and Director of the Department of Institutions of the State of
Louisiana for four years. During this time, my mother began
the Pettit Realty Company. Later, my father joined her in the
business and they are still together in it.

As a boy, I never wanted for anything and that included athletic equipment. I always had everything I needed, but my dad never pushed me about playing sports. He would play catch with me sometimes but he never forced me to be an athlete, even though he was one himself and I knew he would like me to take part in sports.

Actually, he didn't have to push me. I loved all sports and I played them all. That is, I tried to play them. Being an only child, I had no older brothers to help me and no younger brothers to play with, so I would play with the boys in the neighborhood.

I was not very small, but I was thin and frail and I had the coordination of a broomstick. I was not a good athlete—I could not run fast—I was not strong. Whenever they would choose sides for a game, I was always the last boy picked, which, as you can imagine, does very little for your confidence.

I didn't have instruction of any kind in sports; no Little League or anything like that. We didn't have organized teams in grammar school, we simply played before school and during recess. No matter what we played—baseball, football or basketball—the other boys were always better than me.

I was very conscious of it, particularly during my freshman and sophomore years in high school. I had started to spring up and I was well aware that I was taller than most of the other boys. I was also more awkward.

The only thing I can remember being good at was marbles. I was a very good marble shooter.

I went out for football in my freshman year in high school. I was 5' 7" and 118 pounds, which was more of a figure than a build. I wasn't coordinated and I wasn't any good. But I did have desire. More than anything else, I wanted to be a good athlete.

My greatest ambition at that time was to win a high school letter. I had no dreams of playing first string or being a star. All I wanted to do was get enough time in to win a letter because I had a great desire to wear that green and gold-lettered sweater of Baton Rouge High.

I went out for football in my freshman year and they put me on as a third string tackle at 118 pounds. I was sent in for one game as a right tackle on defense, but I lined up as a left tackle instead and they went right through where I was supposed to be for a 65-yard touchdown. That ended my football career.

I went out for baseball and I got in to play second base one time and the guy hit a ball to me and it went right through my legs. That ended my baseball career.

I also went out for track, but I was too slow and uncoordinated.

As a sophomore, I decided to concentrate on basketball. It was the same story and about all I was able to accomplish was to immortalize my high school basketball coach, Kenner Day. I was one of 17 boys to try out for the team and it was Coach Day's job to pick 12. I was not one of the 12 and today, when they introduce him at banquets or write about him in the paper, they say, "here is the man who cut Bob Pettit from his team."

Everybody laughs at that and maybe it embarrasses Coach Day because it makes him appear as if he does not know very much about basketball. I do not feel that way. On the contrary, the fact that he cut me has always indicated to me what a wise and perceptive coach he was. I didn't deserve to make the team. He knew it and truthfully, I knew it too.

Chapter 3 ● UNWANTED ● How can you describe the hurt you feel when you are 14 years old and not good enough to make the team? It is the end of the world. You feel like a failure. You think everywhere you go people are looking at you and pointing a finger and talking about you in whispers. And you hang your head and walk in shame and humiliation.

It hurts to be unwanted—even if it is only by the high school basketball coach. I became the butt of everyone's jokes. One day a bunch of football players came back from practice and took three of us and shaved our heads. I tried to fight them off, but I just wasn't strong enough.

You don't have much choice when you have reached the point where you are not wanted by the team. You can either quit or fight harder. At first I just kind of moped around the house. Then I started to go down to my church, St. James Episcopal, and I began talking to my pastor, Mr. Philip Werlein. I had always been active in church affairs. I sang in the choir, took up collections at services and served as an altar boy.

A bunch of the guys got together and we formed a three-team church league. All the players in the league were, like me, high school basketball dropouts. If you think the NBA is rough, you should have seen those games. This was the first organized basketball I ever played, although disorganized is a better word for it.

Still, I was a member of a team and that made me feel very important. It made all of us feel important. So important, we would show up at the gym and if there was someone on the court, we would shoo them off insisting, "We have to practice for the big game."

There was always this one kid on the court whenever we got there. He was a few years younger and smaller and he loved basketball more than anything else in the world. We would come along and we would tell him to scat and sometimes he refused and a couple of the boys would pick him up bodily and toss him off the court. I doubt if they could do that now. His name is Jimmy Taylor and he plays fullback for the Green Bay Packers.

The church league games were so rough, I had to learn to defend myself. If a guy pushed me, I pushed right back. Once, the referee failed to show up for a game so we went out on the street and asked the first man we saw if he would like to referee the game for two dollars. He said he would.

But he didn't know a thing about basketball and the game got out of hand. When it was over, we all scattered in different directions and the man never got his two dollars.

There were three fellows playing in the church league who have had a lasting place in my life. On one of the teams was Randall Goodwin, who is now my partner in the insurance business and Ned Clark, who played with me for two years in high school and for three years at LSU.

Ned and I used to have vicious battles in the church league but we became roommates at LSU and Ned was the best man at my wedding.

Another friend was Larry Brooks, who was my teammate in the church league and was in my wedding party.

I began to get a little more cocky. That was because I became a regular on the team and I was improving all the time. I was now a part of something and I wanted to make a contribution, so I would practice every chance I got and it soon paid off.

I started practicing at home by bending a wire coat hanger and putting it over the garage door and shooting tennis balls at it. My Dad noticed me and was so pleased I had taken an interest in the sport he went out and bought me a backboard and a basketball. I began a routine which I followed for seven years and this, more than anything, was responsible for helping me improve my game.

I would get home from shool and shoot baskets from 3:30 to 5:30. Then I would have dinner and do my lessons and by 7:30, I was out shooting baskets again. With light from a couple of window lamps, which I placed on the window sill facing the backyard, I was able to practice a few hours at night.

You would be surprised how far you can go with constant and regular practice. It turned me into the leading scorer on my church league team, which may not sound like much, but only a year before I couldn't hold a basketball properly.

I learned a great deal during this period of constant practice. I learned that just about anybody can become a good shooter with regular practice and by following a few simple rules.

Have you ever thrown darts? If so, then you have the fundamental principles of shooting a basketball. There are certain musts in shooting and a well-grounded foundation will eliminate the chance of picking up bad habits. When I started, I waded through a trial-and-error period and picked up so many bad habits, it took me quite awhile to get straightened out.

Here are three rules which head my list:

1. The shoulder, elbow and hand should form a straight line toward the basket when shooting.
2. The elbow should be directly under the ball at all times and should point at the basket throughout the shot.
3. The thumb should be behind the ball and in line with the other four fingers and not under the ball.

Master these three and you will have a sound foundation in shooting. Too many young players have a tendency to let the elbow drift out from under the ball. The best way to check this is to have the elbow touch your side as you begin the shooting motion. Some shooters hold the ball high over their head, others hold it low, that's O.K. The important thing is not to let the elbow drift out.

I hold the basketball in a cradle formed by the fingertips, inside kuckles and thumb. The palm never touches the ball. In fact, I can remember playing on a dirt court and coming home with nothing dirty but my fingertips. When the ball rests in the cradle the left hand functions as a guide. As the ball is released, the left hand falls away from the ball as the right hand continues on through with the shot.

If you are a right handed shooter, the left hand is not used to get the ball up to the basket, merely to steady the ball. The thumb and forefingers line up side by side behind the ball, the spread depending on the individual. I feel too wide a spread hampers a shot but the vital thing is that the thumb stay behind the ball, not under it.

I am not the only example of a person who made it in professional basketball with hard work instead of innate ability. Bob Cousy was not a great player as a boy and neither was Neil Johnston. George Mikan was cut from the squad at Notre Dame before he transferred to DePaul. Paul Arizin first proved himself in an Industrial League when he was a sophomore at Villanova.

All these players are examples of great desire and determination; the hunger to improve and do well was so great it pushed them into greatness. Take Jack Twyman of the Cincinnati Royals. He went out for his high school team as a freshman and was cut. The same thing happened in his sophomore and junior years. Still grimly determined, he went out again as a senior and not only made the team, he became all-state in Pennsylvania and won a basketball scholarship at the University of Cincinnati.

When I look back, the greatest thing that ever happened to me is that when I first picked up a basketball I was terrible. If things come naturally, you may not bother to work at improving them and you can fall short of your potential.

On the other hand, if you are bad, you could say, "What the heck, why should I embarrass myself? I'll never get any better." It is so easy to quit. I am happy I didn't.

The one thing my lack of ability did not break was my spirit. In fact, it made me more determined to play, so after my sophomore year, I went to a boys' camp at Lake George, in upstate

The incorrect way to hold the ball—never let the ball rest in your palm.

The *correct* way to hold the ball—your hand is a cradle formed by the fingertips, inside knuckles and thumb.

Front View

The three basic rules of shooting:
A   The shoulder, elbow and hand should form a straight line.
B   The elbow should be directly under the ball at all times and should point at the basket throughout the shot.
C   The thumb should be behind the ball and in line with the other four fingers and not under the ball.

Side View

Action picture against the Lakers illustrating the proper shooting form. Note the ball—it's cradled on my fingers and thumb and you can see the space between ball and palm. The elbow is pointed straight at basket. (Cast on left arm is for broken wrist suffered against the Celtics.)

New York, called Camp Dudley, where I did nothing but play basketball for six weeks.

I could feel myself getting better and I could see myself getting bigger. By the time I was ready to go back to school, I had sprouted five inches and now stood 6' 4". I began to fill out, too, and I suddenly realized why.

In my freshman year I had developed the habit of doing daily exercises. Every night I would stand on the back steps and hold on to the screen door and do calf rises to build up my legs. Then I would go inside and grab window shade weights and do curls to build up my arms.

I could hardly wait for the basketball season to start in my junior year. I had the confidence because I knew I had the ability to make the team and become one of the boys. I went out for the team and Coach Day was not there because he was assistant football coach and never picked up the basketball team until early December. He turned the team over to Charles Roberts, one of the players, until he was ready to take over.

We would practice every day and scrimmage once a week and Charlie started playing me at center because of my height. I played pretty well in the scrimmages and we were winning each week and Charlie reported to Coach Day. After one good scrimmage, Charlie reported and the coach said, "Who played center?"

"Pettit," Charlie Roberts said.

"Bob Pettit," Coach Day said, unbelievingly, "it can't be. Why, last year he wasn't good enough to stay with the jayvee."

But when Coach Day joined us, he let me stay at center and I stayed there all season. I became one of the boys and I had something to occupy my time, which was another break. Let me explain that at Baton Rouge High, if you played a sport, you would not have to take a physical education class. So, when I was dropped from the basketball team in my sophomore year, they gave me PE in my second period.

If it was a nice day we were supposed to go outside and play ball or something and pretty soon we stopped playing ball because some of the fellows started to bring a deck of cards to school. Another brought a pair of dice and one enterprising young man even brought a roulette wheel. We would spend our physical education period playing black jack and poker and shooting dice behind the bleachers and one morning we had this big dice game going and unbeknown to us, the coaches were watching us from an upstairs window.

Well, before you knew it, three of the coaches surrounded us. Immediately everybody grabbed books and tried pretending they had been studying the whole time, but they didn't fool anybody. One of the boys looked up and saw the coaches coming and in one motion he grabbed his shirt by the lapel, ripped it off and ran for the track as if he had been working out all period.

I had the dice. When I saw the coaches I tossed them into the air and they landed in the wood bleachers and rolled up there and made a noise like a bomb exploding. I was taken to the principal, Miss Alexander, and she said, "Bob, I know your family and if they ever caught you doing something like this there is no telling what they would do."

Of course she was right and when she gave me a choice of punishment—a whipping or two weeks suspension—I gladly took the whipping because then I wouldn't have to tell my parents. Miss Alexander and making the basketball team cured me. I had started to enjoy the little second period sessions and there is no telling where they might have led.

I made the team in my junior year and it even helped me overcome my shyness with girls. On some of our trips we were allowed to bring girls and on one trip there was this one girl I wanted to ask, but I didn't have the nerve. I told one of my friends to invite her along to a tournament we were playing in Zachary, Louisiana. This was my chance to impress her. I was sitting in the bleachers in my warm-up suit waiting for another game to end so that we could take the court. I was wearing this black knit skull cap and she was sitting two rows in front of me. When it came time for us to take the court, I took off my cap and turned and threw it to her and said, "Here, baby; hold this for me." And as I threw it, I lost my balance and fell six rows down the bleachers. Nothing was hurt except my feelings. Some impression I made.

In my junior year we won the city championship and I was named on the All-City team, which wasn't much because there were only two other high schools in Baton Rouge. But to me it was like making All-America.

I had a high game of 32 points and I was shooting the ball much better. I was gaining in confidence and I didn't mind the roughness any more. One game against Istruma High, things got very rough. I was getting pushed around quite a bit and I vowed the next guy who came near me would get it.

The next guy who came near me I saw too late was a boy named Don Dedon. I just swung around and my elbow hit him in the mouth and he just smiled and spit out his six front teeth . . . one . . . two . . . three . . . four . . . five . . . six. I felt terrible and I apologized, but he just shrugged it off with a smile . . . a toothless smile. After all, he was my teammate.

My junior year ended and I finally won my lettered sweater . . . the first letter I ever won. It gets pretty hot in Louisiana in May and June and I got that sweater in May and hot or not, I was going to wear it. I worked too hard for that thing to hang it in a closet.

I had grown a few more inches that summer and when I reported for my senior year, I was almost 6′ 7″. In the beginning of the year, we won 8 and lost 3, then I got the mumps. While I was out, the team lost 9 games, but when I returned we won 17 in a row, including the state championship.

I will never forget one incident during the state tournament. It was in our first game against Fortier High. I scored only about five points in the first half and we were losing at halftime and Coach Day walked into the dressing room, picked up a towel, wet it and hit me as hard as he could across the head with the wet towel. "You get out there and show me something this half," he said. Then he walked out and went directly to my Mom and Dad, who were sitting in the stands, and told them what he did. My Dad said, "Fine."

I was so angry, I went out and scored 20 points in the second half and we won the game and, went on to win the state championship. I have always remembered what Coach Day did and respected him for it because I know it hurt him more than it did me.

I averaged 19 points a game that year with a high of 41 and I was invited to play in the North-South All-Star High School game in Murray, Kentucky. They had invited the best high school players in the North to play against the best in the South and I was very flattered to be chosen to play.

On my team were Dick Rosenthal, who later went to Notre Dame and Tom Marshall, who had a long career in the NBA with the Cincinnati Royals. On the North squad were Togo Palazzi, who became All-America at Holy Cross; B. H. Born, at Kansas and Chuck Noble, who played with the Fort Wayne Pistons.

I scored nine points that night and rebounded well and I was selected on the Chuck Taylor High School team.

When I graduated from Baton Rouge High I had offers from about fourteen schools, but all the while I knew where I wanted to go. I knew where I wanted to go from the time I was a little boy but I never thought I would make it. It just shows what hard work and determination can do because that September I enrolled at Louisiana State University on a full basketball scholarship.

Chapter 4 ● BIG MAN ON CAMPUS ● I was no stranger to Louisiana State University, since Baton Rouge is my home. Besides, when they were trying to help me make my decision to attend school there—a decision I actually had made many years earlier—coach Harry Rabenhorst had some of the boys on his team show me around the campus. So the campus and many of the students were familiar to me.

Still, a certain feeling came over me when I started for school that first day in September 1950. Maybe it was anxiety, maybe it was excitement, maybe it was anticipation. Whatever you call it, it was a strange, almost exhilarating feeling.

I had not yet reached my 18th birthday and I was 6' 8" and still a little gawky and stringy at about 175 pounds. Fortunately, I was well received by the upper classmen. Some I knew from high school, many of them had been opponents in basketball, others were friends from my neighborhood and many of them had read about me in the papers. I was going there with a reputation for basketball potential that would be hard to fulfill.

The freshman team had a 10-game schedule, most of which were played as the preliminary to the varsity games. The freshman coach and assistant varsity coach was John Chaney and he was the first person who ever showed me moves out of the pivot. I had played with my back to the basket all through high school without anyone really showing me what I was doing wrong or how to do it right. John spent a lot of time with me.

I had a little jump shot and a hook shot, which I developed

21

between my senior year in high school and my freshman year in college. I was rebounding well at both ends of the court and John Chaney showed me a move which was to help me immensely. He taught me to fake a jump shot or hook shot when I had my back to the basket, then, when the defensive man committed himself, I would drive around him for an easy layup.

Too many pivot men shoot falling away from the basket, but I developed a shot in which I leaned into the basket. This gives you a tremendous edge. For one thing, you are closer to your target. For another, you are in a position to follow up a missed shot for a rebound or a tip-in and there is a much greater possibility of being fouled in the act of shooting or after the shot.

As a freshman, I averaged over 30 points a game and the team won 8 of the 10 games. This was the year I made my greatest progress. During the summer I worked as a counselor at the Lookout Mountain Camp for Boys in Mentone, Alabama. I spent all my free time practicing my shooting and that is where I developed my hook shot. I was looking forward eagerly to my first college varsity season.

The year before, the regular center at LSU was a boy named Byron Johnson, who stood 6' 10". Since coach Rabenhorst wanted to take advantage of all that height, he had Byron and me play a double pivot. The other big man in the front line was Ned Clark, my church league friend. I started using my big, sweeping hook shot, backing into the basket; I was very successful with it. The team won 17 and lost 7 and I finished with a scoring average of 25.5 in my rookie season. It placed me third in the nation. Clyde Lovellette of Kansas was first with 28.4 points a game and Dick Groat (the Philadelphia shortstop) of Duke averaged 26.0. Both of them were seniors so I figured I had a good shot at leading the country in scoring my junior year.

During my sophomore year, I learned one very valuable lesson from Joe Dean, a senior, who was a guard on the team. There may have been players with more talent but I have never known a player with more confidence than Joe Dean possessed.

"Bob," he told me once, "you are only as good as you think

The champions of Baton Rouge, Louisiana. My junior year in high school. My teammates are (left to right): #4, Donald Dedon; #2, Charles Robert; Coach Kenner Day; #12, myself (isn't that some smile!); #1, R. J. Bourgeois; and #11, Ned Clark. We had the same team the next year and won the state title.

A publicity picture. I was a senior at Louisiana State University and All America.

Making a hook shot against Mississippi. I always played the pivot in college.

The 1954 Eastern All-Star team. This may be the best college all-star team ever assembled. Seated (left to right): Frank Ramsey; Coach Howie Cann; myself; Lou Tsioropoulos; Togo Palazzi. Standing (left to right): John Clune; Bill Hannon; Jerry Domershick; Larry Costello; Al Larkin; Richie Guerin; Cliff Hagan.

you are. Anytime you walk on that basketball court you have to think that you are the best player out there. You cannot believe there is anybody better than you or that anybody can stop you."

Joe Dean was right. It just goes back to the point that the mental aspect of basketball is 50 percent of the battle. That doesn't mean you have to go around telling everybody how great you are. You must be confident without being cocky.

I took Joe Dean's lesson with me and tried to apply it to everything I did. It almost got me in trouble at Camp Lookout that summer. The owner of the camp called me into his office one day. "Bob," he said, "I believe you think too much of yourself. I have a feeling you think you're too good."

"Well," I replied, "you're right because every time I walk out on the basketball court I think I am the best." Joe Dean would have been proud of me.

We had a great team in my junior year. We were undefeated in 14 Southeastern Conference games but there was one disappointment for the boys. The year before, we lost out in the Conference playoff by one point to Kentucky. In my junior year we thought we had the team to beat powerful Kentucky, but the Wildcats were suspended by the NCAA that year. They didn't play a schedule, all they did was practice.

In any event we finished with a 22-1 record and it didn't matter that my average slipped to 24.7 and I fell from third in the country to tenth. I was out of action for four games in January because of a bout with pneumonia. The team won all four games without me. We went to the regional playoffs in Raleigh, North Carolina, and met Lebanon Valley of Pennsylvania in our first game. We beat them, 89-76.

Next we came up against a fine Holy Cross team with Togo Palazzi and a good-looking freshman named Tom Heinsohn. We beat Holy Cross, too, by eight points and now we were in the finals. We flew to Kansas City and on the first night we were to play Indiana, one of the most powerful teams in the country. Their biggest man was All-America Don Schlundt, who was 6' 10" and he and I both scored 29 points that night. The guy who killed us, though, was Bob Leonard. In the first quarter he must have made 10 out of 10 jump shots. They beat us 80-67. Indiana went on to beat Kansas by one point for the NCAA title and we faced Washington for third place.

I never saw a college team as big as Washington. Their center was Bob Houbregs, who was 6' 8". Dean Parsons was one forward and he was also 6' 8" and they had about four players who weighed more than 240. I can remember I did one of my "stellar" defensive jobs against Houbregs. He scored 42 points, mostly with the longest hook shot I have ever seen. They beat us, 88-69.

Those two games in Kansas City were a let-down after a great season and I think they affected us the following year because we had exactly the same team and our record was not as good. Personally, I had my best year as a senior. As a junior, we ran into a lot of zone defenses and that hurt my scoring, but I was really scoring as a senior.

In fact, I was involved in a red hot race with Frank Selvy of Furman for the national scoring championship. Frank had won the scoring championship the year before with an average of 29.5 per game, which was an all-time record. Now, he and I were going at it hot and heavy, both of us scoring at a pace which would break his record and the newspapers were playing up the battle pretty good.

I was averaging a little over 30 points a game to Selvy's 32. On February 13, we played Georgia Tech and I scored 46 points and I remember thinking to myself, "Top that, Frank Selvy." I couldn't wait to see the next day's papers to see where that put me. Furman had played Newberry the night before and I mentally conceded Selvy 30 points, which still might put me ahead of him. You can imagine the shock I received when I picked up the paper the next morning and read that Frank Selvy had scored 100 points. From then on he pulled away and I never could catch him. He set an all-time collegiate scoring record of 41.7 points per game. I was second with 31.4, which would have been good enough to win the title any year but that one.

Frank was a great shooter and he made the pros but he never

approached the potential he had in college until his last three years with the Lakers. He was a forward in college at 6' 3", which made him too short for that position in the pros. He worked at learning the guard spot, eventually mastered it and became one of the best.

We finished 14-0 in the Southeastern Conference again but this time we had to meet Kentucky, also unbeaten, for the right to represent our conference in the NCAA tournament. Even greater than my rivalry with Selvy that year was my rivalry with Cliff Hagan, the Kentucky center, who stood only 6' 4". We had both been selected at center on a number of pre-season All-America teams and the rivalry stemmed from the fact we were in the same conference. I held the Conference scoring record of 50 points and Cliff broke it when he scored 52 that year. Three nights later, I scored 60 points against Louisiana College to regain the record.

Kentucky beat us in the playoff game on a neutral court in Nashville, Tennessee by 4 points in one of the finest games I was ever in, but they decided to pass up the NCAA playoffs and we went instead. We went to the regional playoffs at Iowa City, Iowa, and met up with Penn State, which had an All-America named Jesse Arnelle. They used a pressing zone defense, something I had never seen before and it so rattled us, we were eliminated in our first game.

The year was over for our team, but not for me. I was selected to play in a number of college All-Star games around the country. One was in Kansas City and I was on the West team which beat the East; I was selected Most Valuable Player in the game. We went on to New York and I played on the East team, which may have been the greatest college All-Star team ever assembled. The guards were Frank Selvy and Frank Ramsey, the forwards were Togo Palazzi and Cliff Hagan and I was at center. On the bench were Richie Guerin and Larry Costello. We were supposed to roll right over the West All-Stars, but they surprised us and won the game, and that man, Bob Leonard, did it again. He scored 21 points and was named Most Valuable Player.

The pros scouted that game pretty thoroughly and I got calls from several professional clubs checking on my availability for the NBA. I said certainly I was available but I made no commitments. I said I might be interested in playing pro ball and wanted to know what they had to offer. When the draft came, the first pick went to the Baltimore Bullets, who chose Frank Selvy. The Milwaukee Hawks were next and they picked Bob Pettit. I hadn't even met Ben Kerner, the owner of the Hawks.

I was invited to go on a tour of the country playing against the Harlem Globetrotters. Frank Selvy also was invited and he went because the money was pretty good. So good I was tempted to go, too, but I finally decided against it. If I went, I would be a professional and I would have had no choice but to sign with the Hawks. I had received a few good offers from the top amateur teams like the Phillips Oilers and the Peoria Caterpillars where you work for the company and also play ball. I wanted to maintain my amateur standing and my bargaining position with Mr. Kerner, as well.

I went back to Louisiana State to finish up and get my degree in Business Administration and I waited to hear from Mr. Kerner. Meanwhile, I visited some of the amateur teams and listened to their offers without making any commitment. I had a cousin, Frank Brian, who had played professional ball for Mr. Kerner, so I called Frank and tried to get a line on the owner of the Milwaukee Hawks. Frank was high in his praise of Mr. Kerner.

"Anything he tells you, you can believe," Frank said. "He has a reputation for firing coaches and trading ball players around, but he has to do that to stay in business."

I started weighing possibilities and opportunities and began to realize that if I signed with a professional team I would still be free the rest of the year to work at home. With the amateur team, I'd have to work full time elsewhere. I made up my mind that I'd go with the Hawks if I could work out a good contract.

Finally, in July, Mr. Kerner called and invited me to Milwaukee to see him. He took me out to dinner and we sat around talking basketball and I told him of the fine offers I had from several amateur teams, which included opportunities for a career in business. I knew the Hawks could not match the job security I would get in amateur ball, but I told Mr. Kerner I would play professional ball if the contract were suitable and I was anxious to hear what he had to offer.

We left the restaurant and went to Mr. Kerner's hotel and began dickering for a contract. I was a twenty-one-year-old, inexperienced kid without a lawyer and Mr. Kerner, an experienced, hardened, business man. It was quite a session for me.

Mr. Kerner asked me what I wanted and I said $15,000 and Mr. Kerner said he couldn't possibly pay me $15,000. He said he was thinking of $9500 which equaled the most ever paid a rookie. Mel Hutchins received this.

We kept talking, and finally Mr. Kerner said that he would make it $11,000—at that time a new high for a rookie. This is the figure we finally agreed on, but I held up the signing until I was able to contact the amateur teams I had spoken to and advise them of my decision. I didn't think it would be fair for them to learn about it from the newspapers.

I realized Mr. Kerner's offer of $11,000 was a very generous one since there was no way of knowing how good a professional player I would be. I had only $100 in the bank when I graduated from college and $11,000 looked like all the money in the world to me.

I returned to Baton Rouge, advised the amateur teams of my decision, and telephoned Mr. Kerner that I was now ready to sign the contract and join him.

Mr. Kerner said he was delighted and then he asked me if I would come to Milwaukee about a month ahead of the season so that he could put me to work selling tickets. I said I would be there as soon as I could.

Chapter 5 ● ROOKIE ● In those days the basketball season started around the first of October, but I arrived in Milwaukee a month earlier to help out with the Hawks' ticket sale. It was pretty rough. I worked with a young fellow named Phil Casper, who was half of Mr. Kerner's office staff—the other half was Mr. Kerner's secretary, Pat Fitzgerald.

We called on national organizations, local business people and season ticket holders from the previous year. We had very little success. The Braves had just moved from Boston and everything in town was baseball . . . baseball . . . baseball. Basketball was nothing.

Back home I had known a fellow who went to LSU and was playing with the Braves. He was Joe Adcock, the first baseman, and I looked him up as soon as I could and we renewed our friendship. Joe and I spent a lot of time together and when the baseball season was over I sublet his apartment, which overlooked Lake Michigan.

During the time I was trying to sell tickets, I lived in a hotel and every night Mr. Kerner would take me out to dinner—on him. One night we were having dinner—for about the fifteenth night in a row—and I could tell there was something disturbing him because he wasn't talking as much as usual.

"Bob," he said, finally, "tell me, can you play basketball . . . ?"

Our training camp that year was at Wayne University in Detroit and we reported at the end of September. Red Holzman was the coach and I will always be grateful to him because he made me a forward. He had Charlie Share at center and he

33

felt my build and my style of play were best suited for the forward position. When I reported to camp I was 6′ 9″ and weighed 205.

As a forward, I had to learn the game of basketball all over. Very little of what I knew then was applicable in the pros because in the past I played with my back to the basket and only about 12 feet from the hoop. Now I was facing the basket and was 18 feet away and I had none of the moves which are a must for a forward.

Now, more than ever, I had to rely on my jump shot and it was a lucky thing I had spent so much time perfecting it. Although I did not use it to any great extent in college, the jump shot soon became my most frequent weapon in the pros.

When you talk about the jump shot, you talk about the thing that revolutionized the game. Today every player must have a "jumper."

All the great jump shooters in the NBA feel comfortable when they shoot. It is wrong to copy someone else's style. In jump shooting the stance is up to the individual. I like to crouch slightly, my feet about 12 inches apart. As I jump, I hold the ball with a firm grip and look through the hoop at the back part of the rim.

My right hand, at the start of the jump, is behind the ball and, as I go up, it goes under the ball as I cock my wrist just before releasing the shot. Some shooters make the mistake of jumping too high and pressing too much when they should be relaxed. I release the ball just before I reach the peak of my jump because I don't want to hang in the air and strain.

By releasing the ball slightly before the peak of the jump, your body is behind the ball and it is easier to reach the basket with accuracy.

The same principle applies to jumping into your shot. Watch the accurate jump shooters and you'll notice none of them fall away from the basket as they release the ball.

By moving into his shot, the shooter expends less energy, he's closer to the target and he's in a better position to go to the boards. The jump shooter should not only move into his shot, he should guard against swaying to the right or left. It's easy to check this by noting where you come down after shooting. Your feet should come down on top of your takeoff position or be slightly forward of your takeoff position—not to the right or left or behind it.

When the shot is released, the ball should spin back toward you, not sideways. If the ball does not spin directly back toward you, you're shooting wrong! Your fingertips should be the last thing to leave the ball, your arm should wind up fully extended with your palm facing the floor.

It's possible to practice shooting at home. A mirror can help check your form and throwing objects at a waste paper basket will help improve accuracy and judgment of distance. I have shot at garbage cans and circles with any object I came across, the idea being that anything you do to perfect your rhythm is beneficial.

At first, driving was my biggest problem in the pros because I neglected dribbling as part of my game. As a center, the ball came to me and I just bounced it once and shot. Now I had to learn to drive around my man, which required a good deal of dribbling. I worked hard at it, but all through my career, I never could master the dribbling art.

I also had to learn to maneuver without the ball. I had to start learning to work with the guards. Instead of being fed the ball, I was now required to do the feeding.

In feeding the pivot, with the man guarding him usually playing to one side, I worked at making my pass to the pivot's left or right, away from his defensive man. I always ask the pivot man to give me a target to aim for by holding out his hand where he wants me to pass the ball.

I found also that the lob pass to the pivot man is the worst pass in basketball. Not only is a lob easy to deflect, but the pivot has to surrender his position to get it. I began to concentrate on quick wrist-snap passes and bounce passes, always using the pivot man's hand as a target.

Forwards in high school and college too often overlook the value of moving without the ball. When my team has the ball,

The biggest weapon in my arsenal of shots is the jumper. When you talk about the jump shot, you're talking about the shot that has revolutionized basketball. In these pictures you see different action pictures of my shooting. The first four emphasize the proper grip and arm position. The last four illustrate the follow through.

As I jump, I hold the ball with a firm grip and look through the hoop at the back part of the rim.

Mack Giblin

My right hand, at the start of the jump, is behind the ball and, as I go up, it goes under the ball as I cock my wrist just before releasing the shot.

Even though I have a broken left wrist, as long as the basic principles of shooting are followed, I can still score.

Mack Giblin

I release the ball just before I reach the peak of my jump because I don't want to hang in the air and strain.

By releasing the ball slightly before the peak of the jump, your body is behind the ball and it is easier to reach the basket.

The jump shooter should not only move into his shot, he should guard against swaying to the right or left. It's easy to check this by noting where you come down after shooting.

When the shot is released, the ball should spin back toward you, not sideways. Your fingertips should be the last thing to leave the ball; your arm should wind up fully extended with your hand facing the floor.

I never stand still. If the ball is on the other forward's side of the court, I jockey for position, taking my defensive man toward the baseline so I will be in position to move out and take a pass. Or, I'll try to get in position inside my defensive man in case a shot is taken from the other side of the court. Because the ball is on the other side of the court, it does not mean you are out of the play.

The man who stands still is an easy mark for a defensive man. Not only will an immobile forward have passes taken out of his hands, he will also permit his defender to double team the pivot. By keeping on the move, I can have possession of the ball with my defensive man coming at me. When he drops off, I receive a quick pass and when he comes at me, he's at my mercy because he is moving toward me and I can drive around him.

It is important to remember that winning basketball is the result of five men receiving help from one another. Don't try to get the job done alone.

Another problem I had was learning to play defense on a forward. I had always played a pivot man who was usually stationary. Now I was expected to play a high-scoring forward who could drive, was a good shooter and much more mobile than the players I had guarded in college. I was pretty bad in camp my rookie year and one night Mr. Kerner called in Red Holzman and asked how I was getting along.

"Ben," Red said, "he sure can shoot, but his defense is horrible and his rebounding is worse!" Mr. Kerner didn't sleep well that night.

Red was right and I soon realized I had to work on improving both of these phases of my game. I gradually began to realize rebounding is the most important single factor in winning a basketball game. I've looked at enough rebounding sheets after a game to know 90 percent of the games are won or lost on the boards.

When people ask the secret of being a good rebounder, I say first you have to enjoy it. I've seen big, strong men who can't rebound because they are shy under the boards. To be a good rebounder you have to think big . . . think strong.

Rebounding is another part of basketball where mental attitude is important. Shooting, to a certain degree, is a God-given talent, but I've seen many ordinary athletes think their way into becoming great rebounders. Harry Gallatin was one. I wasn't an exceptional rebounder in high school or college, but as I grew older I became stronger and my desire to mix under the boards increased. I began to take pride in rebounding and worked diligently with weights to increase my strength and jumping ability.

Because it is a challenge, there is nothing I enjoyed better in basketball than rebounding. When I go up for the ball, I feel as though no one in the world is going to take it away from me. For my last five seasons, I averaged 17 to 20 rebounds a game. Although Bill Russell and Wilt Chamberlain averaged more, it didn't dampen my enthusiasm when we played against them. It made me work harder. Twice I was able to lead the league in rebounding, and I am convinced that this developed from my mental outlook as well as physical work. I worked by one special rule: I never waited for a teammate to get the rebound. I always went after every one. Centers and forwards who stand around waiting for others to get the ball soon find themselves on the bench.

The first rule in defensive rebounding is never allow your man to get between you and the basket. The second is not to allow anyone to maneuver you too close to the basket. I like to be 7 to 8 feet from the hoop. I've seen players get pushed too far under the basket with the result that the rebound bounced over their heads.

When the ball leaves the shooter's hand, I don't watch it. I watch the man I am guarding. On normal shots from the outside, I know it takes about three seconds before I can rebound, so when my opponent's team takes a shot, I watch which way my man is going. This enables me to beat him to a spot on the floor and to block him out. After he is blocked out; then I turn and go after the ball.

Blocking out is impossible if you watch the ball after it is shot.

I've learned also that a missed shot from one side of the

court usually bounces off the rim or backboard to the other side.

Once I'm in position, I keep my hands in the air to prevent being called for shoving, and to keep them in ready position for quick rebounds.

Any pushing or shoving is done with the hips. I always try to keep hip contact with the man rebounding against me. I take a stance with my legs as wide apart as is comfortable. As I jump, my hip momentum can put my opponent out of the play.

When I jump for the ball, I try to time myself so I catch it at the height of my jump. Timing is important and the best way to perfect it is to throw balls off the backboard, go up and grab them.

When I get the ball, I take a firm grip on it, trying to squeeze it until my hands meet.

In high school, where I was taller than most, I held defensive rebounds over my head. A firm grip was still necessary.

If there's not a big height advantage, it's far safer to come down with your feet spread, elbows away from the body and bring the ball into your chest or stomach. Your elbows, legs and body form a protective shield, preventing an opponent from coming up from behind or from the side and batting the ball out of your hands.

My first commandment in offensive rebounding is whenever I or one of my teammates shoots, I go in after the shot. Like Arnold Palmer attacks a golf course, I attack the boards, the only exception being when it is necessary to drop back and cover the fast break because one of my guards is out of position.

As an offensive rebounder, I classify myself as a grabber as opposed to the tipper. On anything near the hoop, the tipper will try to tip it in on his first try. I like to go up and grab the ball, come down, fake, go up and lay the ball in. You get more free throws this way. Incidentally, I use the backboard on my rebound shots.

I like to vary my method of going to the boards. For the first two seconds, rebounding is nothing more than a little game of one-on-one. The objective is inside position. When I shoot—

or someone on my team shoot—I watch my man and do anything within the rules to get inside him. If I can't get around him, I try to get a little hip contact with him so that I can get my inside arm over his and have a shot at the ball when it comes off the rim. Anything but get caught behind my man.

The pros allow more contact than there is in high school and college so there's some hard battering going on in the NBA. If some players are jarred hard enough, they'll stop coming to the boards. Others, like Tommy Heinsohn and Elgin Baylor, will continue to come in regardless of how hard you hit them.

When I'm shooting, I can tell 90 percent of the time whether the shot will be good or bad when the ball leaves my hand. If it looks like a miss, the moment my feet touch the floor, my first move is to charge in toward the basket. If I can get inside my defensive man, I'll start blocking him out as far as I can by backing up to get contact with him.

The NBA used to have an All-Star game in Chicago before the season began. The rookies in the league would play the defending NBA champions. In 1954, as a rookie, I was invited and I had to interrupt my schooling as a forward to play in the game along with Frank Selvy, Togo Palazzi, Johnny Kerr, Frank Ramsey and Cliff Hagan against the Minneapolis Lakers. It was my first game as a pro and the first time Mr. Kerner saw me play. He must have been sick all night because I scored just three foul shots the entire game.

We went from Chicago to play the Lakers in Minneapolis and then we ended the three-game tour against the Syracuse Nationals in Syracuse before I reported back to camp to continue my education.

We lost all three games, but I played better in the last two than I did in Chicago.

In Syracuse I was assigned to guard Dolph Schayes. I had never seen him play, so I picked him up about 25 feet from the basket, figuring, heck, nobody can hit from out here. I figured wrong because Dolph took the ball and threw in a two-

handed set and I said to myself, "Let me see him do it again."
He did it again, only this time it was from 30 feet out. So next
time I picked him up a little sooner and he grabbed the ball and
threw in a two-handed set from 38 feet out and right away I
learned something about Dolph Schayes. I learned never to
give him his two-handed shot no matter where he was on the
court. Dolph has the best long two-handed shot I ever played
against.

After the game in Syracuse, I flew back to Minneapolis to
join the Hawks, who were playing ten straight exhibition games
against the Lakers in such thriving centers as Wolf Point, Montana, Huron, South Dakota and Anaconda, Montana. We drew
well in these towns. We usually drew more people than lived
in the whole town because people came from surrounding
areas to see us play. What they did was schedule the game
in the largest gym available and we averaged about 2500
spectators per game.

The thing I remember most about the exhibition tour was
the size of the Lakers. The center was Clyde Lovellette, who
was 6′ 9″ and 245 pounds; one forward was Vern Mikkelsen,
6′ 7″, 255 pounds and the other forward was Jim Pollard, who
stood 6′ 6″. This is not big by today's standards, but in their day
the Lakers were gigantic. Their fourth forward was Ed Kalafat
who was 6′ 6″ and weighed 260. George Mikan also played part
of the year and he was 6′ 10″ and 275.

I must digress and say that Jim Pollard was a player who
was born too soon. He was years ahead of his time. Today, he
would be in the super-star class, but he played before the
24-second clock and that hurt his style. He could do everything with a basketball. He was a tremendous outside shooter,
a fine rebounder, a great jump shooter and could dribble as
well as any guard you can name. But the nature of the game
and his team did not call for a fast game and I believe the
deliberate style of the Lakers detracted from Pollard's fame.
I remember in one of these exhibition games I had to pick up
Jim twice as he drove down court. Both times I picked him up
at the top of the keyhole and he went around me like I was
standing still.

The first of our ten exhibitions with the Lakers was in Wolf Point, Montana, in a high school gym. I was warming up when the Lakers took the court, and just looking at the size of them scared me. The toughest and roughest looking of them all was Mikkelsen. I thought to myself, "Well, I'll probably guard Lovellette or Pollard. I want no part of that Mikkelsen." Naturally, Holzman assigned me to Mikkelsen.

For the first half I might as well not have been on the floor; I didn't do a thing. The Lakers just beat me to death. I had no idea of the physical contact that went on under the basket. I was learning the facts of NBA life in a hurry. In my career, I had 125 stitches taken in my face in eleven years in the league. I also had two broken arms, four broken bones in my back, a torn up knee and a torn up stomach. All this in a non-contact sport.

I kind of wandered around in a daze for the first half and at halftime Holzman came up to me and said, "Pettit, tell me this. Do you like playing professional basketball?"

What a question, I thought. I had played one half of one exhibition game. I answered anyway. "Yeah, Mr. Holzman," I said. "I think it's fine. I'm having a real good time."

"Well, let me tell you something, boy," he said. "If you don't go out there and hit the first guy you see coming at you, I'm going to ship you back to Baton Rouge tomorrow."

I said, "Are you serious, Mr. Holzman?"

"Yes," he shouted. "The first guy who comes close to you in the second half I want you to hit with an elbow. You have to get a little aggressive and get these guys off you."

When we went out for the second half, I looked around for the smallest guy on the court and I spotted him. Slater Martin, about 5′ 10″ and 165 pounds. There was my man.

On the first play in the second half, Bobby Harrison threw me a pass on the high post and cut off me and Slater Martin was guarding Harrison. As Slater went by me, I took the ball in both hands and turned around and took a swing with my elbow. Martin went by so fast, I missed him completely and smashed Mikkelsen right in the chest. All of a sudden Mikkelsen looked bigger to me than ever, like he was swelling before

my eyes. I just stood there looking up at him and watching
him look down at me and I felt he could stick out his hand
and crush me like an ant if he wanted to and so I said the
only thing I could think of.

"Please excuse me, Mr. Mikkelsen."

The Lakers gave us a pretty good going over on the exhibition tour and we were happy to open the season. Our first opponent was the Fort Wayne Pistons and I made my professional debut in Milwaukee with one of the finest defensive
forwards in the game guarding me. He was Mel Hutchins.

One of my opponents in my debut was my cousin, Frank
Brian. The Pistons beat us and I broke into the league by scoring 17 points. The next night we played in New York and I
was held to six points and we lost that game, too. It was going
to be an interesting season.

The team was going very bad but in December we acquired
two players who were to leave their mark on professional basketball. The first was Alex Hannum. Alex was owned by the
Rochester Royals, but he held out for the 1954-55 season, the
difference being something like $500. Rather than sign for less
than he felt he deserved, Alex stayed in California working on
construction and finally, after much dickering, the Royals realized Alex' holdout was sincere, so they sold his contract to us.
Mr. Kerner immediately straightened things out with Alex and
he joined us at mid-year.

At about the same time as we were getting Hannum, the
Baltimore Bullets ran into financial difficulty and the team
folded. All their players were up for grabs. Their top player
was Frank Selvy and we got him because, having the poorest
record in the league, we were permitted to pick first. Frank
became our starting guard and did a fine job.

I was sorry to see the Bullets go because I had 35 rebounds
against them in one game—the most I ever got in my life.
When the Bullets folded, my record was stricken from the
books. I also had my first fight in professional basketball against
the Bullets. Paul Hoffman, later general manager of the new
Bullets, and Bobby Harrison got into a squabble and I was

dumb enough to jump right into the middle of it. Before I knew it there were about eight guys pounding me and I was down on my hands and knees looking for a place to crawl out through a sea of legs.

In the middle of my rookie season, I started to play good ball. I was gaining confidence and hitting my jump shot and my hook shot and I was even starting to score points on a drive and rebounding off both boards. I went through one stretch in which I scored 30 or more points seven consecutive nights. I was even getting accustomed to the rough stuff and not minding it very much anymore.

Then in one game against the Rochester Royals in Milwaukee, we were leading by two with five seconds to go and I had one free throw, which would put the game on ice. I missed the shot and Tom Marshall grabbed the rebound, dribbled down court and scored to tie and we lost in overtime. I was feeling pretty low and as I left the floor, I passed in front of Les Harrison, owner-coach of the Royals.

"Thanks for the game, Bob," he said.

Then and there I made up my mind to make him pay for that and from then on I was always "up" for a game against the Royals. The rest of the year I averaged over 30 points a game against them.

We made a tour through the South that year, playing in New Orleans, Shreveport and Baton Rouge. I had no doubt that my presence on the team had something to do with Mr. Kerner arranging the schedule that way. I didn't mind. I was happy to help Mr. Kerner out and I was happy to get home. They had a Bob Pettit night in Baton Rouge and I scored 21 points before 12,000 people, most of them my friends and relatives. The night was quite a success and helped Mr. Kerner get through the season.

We finished last in the Western Division with a record of 26 and 46. We were a poor team and we were practically sneered at in Milwaukee. Actually, Mr. Kerner wouldn't have minded being sneered at, but in truth what we were being was ignored. We were not getting much publicity because everything in the papers was baseball. In retrospect, it is ironic the way things turned out with the Braves leaving Milwaukee for Atlanta and the Hawks becoming a solid franchise in St. Louis.

One night we beat the New York Knickerbockers in Milwaukee for one of our few wins all year. I had a good night and I was expecting to read about the game in headlines the next day. Instead, our game was at the bottom of the third sports page, the worst spot in the paper, under a three-column headline. The main sports headline of that day was "BILLY BRUTON BAGS THREE QUAIL."

In January, Selvy and I were selected to play in the All-Star game in New York. We were the only Hawks chosen and since we were both rookies, it was quite a tribute. Red Holzman didn't want us to go. He figured we were a couple of small town hicks too dumb to get to New York by ourselves. We were to fly from Milwaukee to New York with a stopover in Chicago to spend the night. Red didn't think we were capable of taking care of ourselves, although we were both twenty-two years old and college graduates. Finally, he consented to let us go, but not until he came to me with a worried look in his eyes. He called me Slim and he called Frank and me aside one night.

"Look, Slim," Red said (pronouncing it like it was spelled Schlim) "you and Frankie have to go to Chicago and you have to get a cab from the station to the hotel because you are going to spend the night in the Sheraton-Chicago and you have to be up in the morning and take a cab to the airport and go to the right counter so you will get on the right plane to New York and . . ."

Frank and I listened very carefully and seriously and when Red was finished I asked him, "Now where are we spending the night?" He repeated, "The Sheraton-Chicago." I turned to Selvy and said, "O.K. Frank, you remember Sheraton and I'll remember Chicago."

I averaged 20.4 points a game and was chosen "Rookie of the Year." Between Frank Selvy and me we scored 40 points a game and took most of the shots. Anyone who wanted to shoot had to check with us first. I also made the all-pro team, only the second time a rookie had been selected. The first was Alex Groza.

A lot of players coming out of college want to play with the best and are disappointed if they are selected to play on an also-ran. I believe it was the best break I could have had. I was able to play every minute and work out my mistakes on the floor without the pressure of winning that exists with a contender. I learned in one year what most players learn in five because of all the playing time I had. With another team I probably would have been sitting on the bench with all the mistakes I made. And since I was with a loser, I was in the happy position of having a team built around me, which continued for my entire career. I started with a pro team, became a pretty good player and they built an entire offense around me. This is the greatest compliment any player can be paid.

After my rookie year I went back to Baton Rouge to start my career in the real estate business. During the summer, Mr. Kerner called me and said he was thinking of moving the team to St. Louis. We had played a game there in my rookie year and drew 8,000 against the Boston Celtics and that turnout excited Mr. Kerner. He was certain St. Louis would support professional basketball—at least better than Milwaukee.

Mr. Kerner had lost about $40,000 that year and he was growing desperate. He had borrowed money on the cash value of his life insurance and mortgaged his beautiful home in Buffalo just to keep the team going. He was in debt for $80,000 and he could see no way out but to sell the Hawks, which was the last thing he wanted to do.

Mr. Maurice Podoloff, commissioner of the league, had arranged a sale with a group of businessmen from Washington, D.C. and Mr. Kerner went to New York to meet with them and complete the deal. He took a huge suite in the Waldorf-Astoria to make a good impression on the men. The best offer was $65,000 and Mr. Kerner realized that would still put him $15,000 in debt, so he said nothing doing. He decided to stick it out and returned to Milwaukee with his basketball team and his $80,000 in IOU's.

He knew he had to get out of Milwaukee because the people there just didn't give a hang about basketball. That's when he remembered St. Louis. He flew to St. Louis and in August he called the press together, at a cocktail party, and announced he was moving the Hawks to that city. It was a decision he has never regretted and neither have I because I loved playing in St. Louis. But it wouldn't have been possible were it not for the courage and conviction of Mr. Ben Kerner, and, a little bit of luck.

Chapter 6 ● MR. KERNER ● Just about everything I have in life I owe to basketball. It helped me overcome my awkwardness and self consciousness and it gave me confidence and strength. It put me through college, gave me fame and a good living for many years and helped me establish myself in business to a point where I have financial security few men my age possess.

These are all tangible things and I am grateful to basketball for the intangibles as well. One of them was the opportunity to meet and play for Ben Kerner. I have never known a ball player and an owner to have such a close relationship as I enjoyed with Mr. Kerner in the eleven years I played for him. He always commanded respect, yet I was never conscious of an employer-employee relationship and I am proud to number him among my friends.

I think the NBA is lucky to have Mr. Kerner as an owner. He is a very progressive thinking person, a promotion-minded owner who is always looking for ideas to help sell his product and further the cause of professional basketball. He has staged giveaway nights and variety nights and countless other promotions designed to bring the fan into his arena to watch pro basketball, and for this the league should be grateful.

But what I have always respected about Mr. Kerner is the way he treats his ball players. He has always been more than fair with them. I sincerely believe our players were treated better than any other players in the sport. But in return, he

didn't ask, he demanded they produce on the court. He will
not tolerate losing.

Most teams go to the West Coast twice a season and play
four games each trip. Mr. Kerner would never let us play four
games on any one trip to the coast and usually we would not
play three. We would make an extra two trips although it
would cost him $4,000 or $5,000 in travel expenses each trip.
But San Francisco and Los Angeles were such tough teams he
would never put his team in jeopardy of losing all four games
on one trip. He wanted us to have every opportunity to win,
so he would pay the additional fare.

Several years ago we won four games in a row and we were
about to go out for the fifth when Mr. Kerner entered our
dressing room.

"Make it five straight, boys, and I'll buy everybody a new
sports coat," he said. We won the game and collected the coats
and Mr. Kerner came into the dressing room before the next
game.

"Win tonight," he said, "and you will all get a new pair of
slacks." We won.

"Make it seven in a row and you get new sweaters."

We got the sweaters and eight in a row was for a pair of
shoes and we won that one, too.

"Fifteen in a row," Mr. Kerner said, "and you all get new
cars."

We wound up winning nine straight, then lost, and we didn't
get the new cars, but we each got a topcoat. The tenth game
we lost by one point in overtime, then we won six more in a
row, so if we hadn't lost that one game, we all would have had
new autos. Finally the league made Mr. Kerner put a stop to
the extra incentive, but not before we became the best-dressed
team in the NBA.

Another time we reached the finals of the playoff by beating
Minneapolis for the Western Division championship. We were
about to go out for the start of the series with Boston when
Mr. Kerner visited us. He put his hand in his pocket and pulled
out a piece of paper, which apparently was a check. He threw

it on a table and said, "Boys, whether you win or lose the championship, in my opinion you are champions and I'm going to see that you get the champion's share."

We lost the title, but we actually got more money out of it than the Boston players because we were carrying one less player than they had.

Once, I was passing the Hawks' offices on my way to pick up a new car I had bought. I decided to stop by to say hello to Mr. Kerner.

"Come on in, Bob," he said. "Where are you going?"

"I'm just going down to pick up my new car, Mr. Kerner," I said.

"What did you get?"

"A new Oldsmobile 98, four-door, air-conditioned."

"Really?" he said. "How much will it cost you?"

"I'm trading in my old car, so it will cost about $2,000 in cash."

And he walked to the door and opened it and called for his bookkeeper to come in and just like that he said to the bookkeeper, "Write Bob a check for $2,000. I want to buy him a car as a present."

I have always found Mr. Kerner eminently fair to deal with at contract time. In fact, I learned a lot of business techniques from my bargaining with him over my annual contract.

Most teams in professional sports simply mail their contracts to the players and wait to hear from them by mail. The player either signs his contract or returns it unsigned at which time there is a lot of bargaining, usually by mail. Mr. Kerner operates differently. He calls each of his players to his office for contract talks. I always faced these talks with mixed emotions. On one hand I was frightened of them and on the other, I found them exciting and interesting. I learned as much as I could about business and finance from my talks with Mr. Kerner.

One thing about these talks, they never ended until we came to some agreement. Sometimes, I would come into the room at one in the afternoon and we'd still be talking at seven

The most important thing in rebounding is position. This picture shows perfect position. Note that I have my man on my outside hip, elbows up and knees flexed.

The first thing to do after you've got the ball: Turn and look for the outlet. Here I've got the ball and while in the air I'm beginning to turn and look for my guard to begin the fast break.

You have to really want that ball to be a good rebounder. Here I take one while knocking my teammate over.

The man whose back I'm using as a step ladder is Wilt Chamberlain. At least I was aggressive.

This time I went for the tip. I had good offensive position and got in close for the tip.

One of my favorite pictures—the 1962 All-Star game where I was named Most Valuable Player.

This shows what happens when everyone stands around. This is an
offensive rebound I've taken and the defense didn't block me out nor

Mack Giblin

did it attack the boards. I went right back up for two and was fouled, making a three point play.

that night. We would just sit and bargain and if we reached an impasse, we would change the subject and discuss other things.

With Mr. Kerner I tried never to make the first concession. Say I asked for $25,000 and he was offering $20,000. I would never be the first one to start compromising because if I said $24,000, I knew we would meet somewhere between $20,000 and $24,000. But if I let him come up to $21,000, then we would meet somewhere between $21,000 and $25,000 and I wanted that $1,000. Sometimes we would spend thirty-five to forty minutes just staring out of the window with neither of us willing to budge. At those prices, I could be quiet for a long time.

I never argued with Mr. Kerner over a contract. We would usually sit and talk for a long time and eventually come to some mutual agreement.

Once Mr. Kerner and Jack McMahon were hung up over $500. Finally, Mr. Kerner said, "O.K., Jack, I'll flip you for the $500." Jack nearly had a hemorrhage as he blurted, "Oh, no, I can't do that, I can't do that." Jack got his $500.

Mr. Kerner told me he once was bargaining with a player for a long time and they were still far apart, so Mr. Kerner reached into his desk and pulled out $1,000 in tens and fives and laid it on the desk.

"Sign the contract and this $1,000 is yours," Mr. Kerner said. The player took one look at all that money right before his eyes, signed the contract and picked up the cash and walked out.

I never had a contract with a bonus for attendance or the amount of points I scored because I never wanted to worry about anything but playing my game. I just wanted to be paid on my over-all performance and the success of the team and I can say I was always treated more than fairly.

Mr. Kerner once signed a player on the wing of an airplane. He met a plane as it was passing through town and he and the player sat on the wing and signed the contract while the plane made its stopover.

He got me once in his car as we were driving to the airport. We had been dickering in his office for hours when he suddenly said, "Take a ride to the airport with me, Bob." He promised to pick up Len Koppett of *The New York Times*, who was flying to St. Louis, and on our way to pick up Len, I signed my contract.

Apart from being a great promoter, Mr. Kerner is a tremendous organizer. He has always been wise enough to surround himself with the best men available. In my first year with the Hawks, he made three important acquisitions. One was Alex Hannum and another was Frank Selvy and the third was Marty Blake from Wilkes-Barre, Pennsylvania.

Marty arrived in Milwaukee wearing an orange tie, a pink shirt, a brown coat, blue pants, white socks and saddle oxfords. He had a voice that would shatter an anvil and a cigar that preceded him by half a mile. He claimed to be a combination of Jack E. Leonard and Mike Todd, and came to help Mr. Kerner with some of the work around the ball club because Mr. Kerner couldn't do everything by himself. Since then, Marty has worked his way up to General Manager of the Hawks and is the hardest working man I have ever seen and one of the biggest reasons for the Hawks success. He and I have become close personal friends over the past eleven years.

A lot has been written knocking Mr. Kerner for the way he fires coaches. They say he changes coaches like most people change shirts. In eleven years with the Hawks, I played for nine coaches and none of them lasted as long as three years. Let me say that the only time he fired a coach was when he sincerely believed it was for the good of the team. The last thing he ever wanted to do was fire a coach and he did it only if he thought it would improve the team. I know everybody who worked for him respected him and I will say one thing— they made more money coaching for the St. Louis Hawks as they could have made coaching for any other team.

Mr. Kerner is a man with a great deal of courage. If a decision has to be made, he makes it even in the face of criticism and lets the chips fall where they may. The best example of that came after the 1961-62 season, a disastrous one for the Hawks. Mr. Kerner simply cleaned house. He hired Harry Gallatin as coach and he got rid of nine of the eleven players who were there the previous year and that has to be unprecedented in professional sports where an owner erases 9/11 of a team. The results of the 1962-63 season proved that Mr. Kerner made a wise move.

The relationship I had with Ben Kerner was probably the most unique in sports between owner and player. We were and are very close friends. It will seem strange not to be working for him after eleven years and I'm going to miss our association very much.

Chapter 7 ● THE POLISHED PRO ● After our reception in Milwaukee, we were looking forward to playing in St. Louis. We wanted to make a good showing, partly for Mr. Kerner and mostly for us. If we didn't catch on in St. Louis, many of us would find ourselves out of a job.

We had a good draft that year, picking up Dick Ricketts, Al Ferrari and Med Park and during the season we made a trade which was to figure prominently in the future of the Hawks. We traded Ricketts to Rochester for Jack Coleman and Jack McMahon. They immediately stepped into our starting lineup and did a tremendous job for us and both became two of my favorite people in basketball.

McMahon was a tremendous help to me as a guard; he was totally unselfish and a magnificent playmaker. He was one of the best middle men I have ever seen on the fast break. He wasn't very fast and to me this is one of the secrets of handling the ball in the middle on the fast break—to hold up until your cutters get out on the sidelines, a couple of steps in front of you. Jack would never shoot unless he had to. He was poor on layups and I would get six to eight points a game just tipping in his missed layups.

It was a standing joke that Jack missed more layups than free throws because when he was driving, he never looked at the goal, he looked to feed one of his teammates. When everyone was covered, he'd toss a hope shot. Although I kidded

Jack about his poor percentage on layups, I made it a point to hustle down court when he had the ball, so if he missed, I was there to tip it in.

Shooting layups brings out the worst in some players. They turn into contortionists, twisting their bodies and spinning the ball against the backboard. You should apply the same principle to the layup as you do to a jump shot. Keep it simple, don't get fancy.

I like to go for the goal with a firm grip on the ball and lay it softly onto the backboard with little or no spin. While some like the "hand behind the ball" method, I prefer my hand under the ball, letting it roll off my fingertips as if I'm presenting it to the basket. I feel this helps me protect the ball better, draw more free throws and shoot a softer shot. Young boys just starting, though, should put their hand behind, not under, the ball when shooting layups.

On driving layups, I watch my defensive man, not the goal. However, the second I spring off my left foot, my eye goes to a spot on the backboard I want to hit.

This brings up the question of when to bank a shot off the backboard. I have always followed this simple formula: within four feet or so of the hoop, I shoot for a spot on the backboard. The hardest shot for me is the three or four footer and I feel there is much less margin for error if you bank it since you can slam the ball hard or shoot it softly and still wind up with two points.

While the layup is the desired climax of the fast break, the defensive rebound can be considered the starting point of the fast break. One of my pet peeves is to see a player, once he has cleared the boards, hold the ball too long. The first duty of the defensive rebounder is to protect the ball. The second is to turn and look for a guard for an outlet pass.

The guard also has certain duties and one of the first is a voice signal for the rebounder. The guard should get in position close to the sideline near midcourt, but if you don't get a voice signal, you can lose precious seconds trying to find him. Talking to each other on offense and defense is an important part of teamwork and winning basketball. A shout, a direction, a command makes for quick moves.

The outlet pass should be hard and firm—the one handed baseball pass or the two-handed chest pass, depending on the distance to be covered. The chest pass usually is more accurate at a shorter distance, the baseball pass at a longer distance.

Once the guard receives the pass, he must get the ball to the middle of the court as soon as possible, either by dribbling or passing to the other guard cutting toward the middle. The ball should be in the middle a little beyond midcourt as you start down court.

The three-lane fast break is ideal. The proper position of the cutters is near the sidelines, a step or two in front of the middle man. Unless the middle man has a chance to go in for a layup, he should stop at the foul line and, if the defense retreats to seal off the pass to the cutters, the middle man is free to shoot from the free throw line. If the defense comes up to meet him, a bounce pass to one side or the other usually results in a layup. A bounce pass is much more desirable because there is less of a chance of an interception.

I was in my second year in the league and I was learning more and more each game. By now all these maneuvers—the rebounding techniques, what to do on the fast break, were becoming second nature. But in that second year, I ran into something I hadn't bargained for.

His name was Walter Dukes and he stood 7 feet and weighed 230 pounds. He played for the New York Knicks at the time and he was the roughest ball player I have ever seen. I must have had fifteen fights with Walter through the years and lost them all. I have the greatest respect in the world for Walter because although he would beat me to a pulp when we played, if I hit him he would never say a word. Whatever he dished out, he expected in return.

One story that is told about Walter is that when he was with Detroit, Dukes was playing against the Knickerbockers and guarding a boy named Charlie Tyra and Walter was beating the devil out of Charlie, who was 6′ 7″ and 250 pounds. At one

point, Tyra went for the basket and Wally knocked him to the
floor, fell on top of him, stepped on his stomach, walked back
to the foul line and just stood there with his head back, gazing
at the rafters. Tyra decided he had just about enough. He
slammed the ball on the floor, walked up to Dukes and belted
him right on the jaw as hard as he could. Dukes' head just
went back about two inches and Wally just stood there staring
at Tyra. Charlie Tyra and I were brought up in the same
school—if you hit somebody as hard as you can and he doesn't
fall, then you just better leave the scene of the accident right
quick. That's exactly what Tyra did.

Later, in the dressing room, someone asked Dukes why he
didn't hit Tyra back.

"Well," Walter said, "I didn't think he meant it."

We did fairly well our first year in St. Louis. We made the
playoffs for the first time in many years. I led the league in
scoring with 25.7 points a game and in rebounding and was
named the league's Most Valuable Player for the 1955-56 season. Mr. Kerner said he made a $7,000 profit for the year, which
was not sensational, but was enough to convince him the people of St. Louis would support professional basketball.

That summer there was a trade that had a great effect on
professional basketball. The Rochester Royals had first choice
and picked Sihugo Green of Duquesne. We had the second
draft choice and the Boston Celtics wanted it very much. So
much they were willing to give up the veteran Ed Macauley,
who had been a great player for them for almost 10 years.
Actually, they had no choice because Ed was anxious to return
to his home in St. Louis and he said he would quit the game
if he couldn't play in his home town. So we were able to acquire Ed and, in addition, the Celtics gave us Cliff Hagan in
the same deal.

The man the Celtics wanted was a tall, skinny center, who
was graduating from the University of San Francisco that year.
He was considered an excellent defensive player, but not a very
good shooter. Still, the Celtics were willing to take a chance
on the young fellow, Bill Russell.

I know the Hawks would have liked to have had Russell, but there were too many problems connected with signing him. First, he was on the 1956 Olympic team, which meant he wouldn't be available until the middle of December and would miss the first two months of the season, because the Olympic Games were held in November in Australia.

Second, he was talking about signing with the Harlem Globetrotters.

Third, nobody knew just how good a player he would be.

Fourth, he was certain to ask for a lot of money to sign and Mr. Kerner was not willing to gamble that much on a rookie.

So, the Celtics took on all the headaches of signing Russell and we got one established player and one promising player and you would have to say it was one of the best trades in basketball history because both teams benefited.

Before the season, Marty Blake had arranged a trip for the team to Mexico as a publicity stunt. We were to play seven games in Mexico City and three in Monterey against the Mexico City All-Stars. But the Mexico City All-Stars never materialized and we wound up playing intra-squad games instead.

When we arrived in Mexico, I was greeted by these big life-sized posters of me in my basketball uniform. They were all over the city and underneath it said, "Bob Pettit, *el mas grande jugador del basketbol del mundo.*" Somebody told me it meant "the greatest basketball player in the world."

In Mexico, they had a unique way of introducing teams. You walk on the court and the teams line up on each side and they turn out all the lights in the auditorium, with the exception of a spotlight which is focused on center court. As each player is introduced he runs out and is picked up by the spotlight. Then he turns to each of the four corners of the court and waves. Then he runs to the basket and somebody throws him a ball and he shoots a layup.

Since I was "*el mas grande jugador del basketbol del mundo,*" I was the last one to be introduced and I had arranged to have Bob Schafer, a rookie from Villanova, throw me the ball. I ran out to center court, waved to all four corners, cut toward the basket and waited for Schafer to toss me the ball. He did, but he purposely tossed it behind me and I could barely see it in the darkness. I leaned back to try to catch it and I started to stumble, but I held my balance, grabbed the ball, dribbled to the basket, went up for my layup and hit the bottom of the basket. The ball shot down and hit me in the head.

In Mexico, if they disapprove of something, they whistle and they didn't approve of the first play they had seen by *el mas grande jugador del basketbol del mundo.* You better believe I never heard so much whistling in my life.

The change in diet gave all of us trouble, but one of the newcomers to our squad, Bob Peterson, was particularly unfortunate. On our first night in Mexico City, as our cab was crossing a bridge, Bob asked the driver to stop and he bolted out of the door. When Bob returned, he was greatly relieved, but in the process, his false teeth had fallen into the river. For the next two weeks, until we could get home, poor Bob had a new diet problem—being without teeth.

During the tour a problem arose over Cliff Hagan, who had been such a great center in college, although he stood only 6′ 4″. Red Holzman felt Hagan was too small to play forward, so he tried to convert him to guard. But Cliff was so unfamiliar with the position he just couldn't do the job and he sat on the bench the whole first half of the season. St. Louis tried to sell him to Philadelphia for $1,000, but the Warriors wouldn't buy him. We tried to trade him to Minneapolis for Chuck Mencel. Nothing doing. Nobody wanted Cliff. Both teams lived to regret not making that deal.

After the tour, we made a trade with New York because we were desperately in need of a guard. We gave up Willie Naulls, our first draft choice, in exchange for the veteran Slater Martin. Of all the people I have played with or against, Slater will be the one I remember longest and with the most affection. We became very close friends. He is one of the finest guys I've known. A small man, playing pro ball, 5′ 9″ and 165 pounds, he made up for his lack of height with great desire. When people tell me their son is a great basketball player but is too small, I tell them about Slater. He was a great star in the NBA and he made it on talent and desire. If a boy has the desire and drive and wants to make it, he can make any team at any level. But he has to want it bad enough to make the sacrifice.

One night we were in a small restaurant and a man came up to Slater. The man was obviously intoxicated and he kept needling Slater, saying, "Martin, you stink. You are the worst basketball player around. Why don't you quit?"

Slater tried very hard to keep his head. "Look, sir," he said, "I am here having dinner with some friends. Now why don't you just leave us alone?"

But the guy wouldn't quit. "Who do you think you are, some kind of tough guy?"

"Okay buddy, I know you are looking for trouble," Slater said. "I'll tell you what. Just touch my shoulder, will you?"

The man touched his shoulder and Slater hit him with a right hand and laid him up against the wall.

Everytime I got into a fight, Slater was always in the middle of it. He would usually end up fighting somebody who was 6′ 8″ or so, but it never made any difference to him. The minute any trouble started, he was right there. He was a great guy and for the next three years, he was a tremendous spark to our team.

One night in January, a group of friends came up to St. Louis from Baton Rouge to see us play the Celtics and as I drove in for a layup, I tried to go around Jim Loscutoff and fell on my left wrist and broke it. I had a cast put on immediately.

I broke the wrist on Friday, sat out on Saturday and was sitting on the bench in Minneapolis on Sunday, when Hannum sent me into the game, although my arm was in a cast from my knuckles to my elbow. There were five seconds left and we were leading by a point. I held the ball after it was tipped to

A   Paul Silas (29) comes to the top of the key and sets the pick as I start around Bailey Howell.

B   Howell tries to fight through as I continue around.

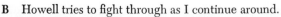

C   Silas holds position as I start final step to begin jump shot.

D   I begin to go up as Silas releases, Howell leaps at me and Bellamy moves up.

Mack Giblin

E My shot is off as Howell hits me and Bellamy misses blocking it. Note Silas cutting to basket. I could, if necessary, have passed to him. The shot was good and Howell was called

me and waited for the gun to go off. In those days there was no such thing as sitting out with an injury. If you could walk, you played, bad hand or not.

Dr. Stan London, our team physician and my close friend, put my arm in a special cast which, when I raised it, left me in shooting position. After two weeks I was playing quite a bit and after five weeks, I was playing full time again. I was pleased with the speed of my recovery, but I was not able to regain the league scoring leadership, which I held before the accident.

One good thing came out of my broken wrist. Hannum started playing Cliff Hagan at forward and Cliff immediately began to do a great job. He averaged 17 points a game for the remainder of the season and became a regular forward. So, my misfortune became Cliff's good fortune, which is the way of the world in professional athletics.

By this time, I had a pretty good reputation and some people might have thought I enjoyed some of the advantages of star status, but this was not true. One player who thought so was a New York rookie named Guy Sparrow. I didn't know him very well and one time I drove for a layup and a foul was called against the defense and Sparrow, who wasn't even in the play, sent up a storm of protest, complaining I was being protected because I was a star. I just turned around and looked at him and said, "Look, rookie, don't talk to me until I know your name."

Bill Russell joined the Celtics in December and for the first few years he was in the league, I found myself matched up against him. I had pretty good success against him, then Red Auerbach made him take the pivot man and he first used Tom Heinsohn, then Jim Loscutoff and finally Tom Sanders to guard me and this is when I began having trouble with Russell. If I would get by Heinsohn or Sanders or Lusky along would come Russell to stop me. What made it difficult was that I never knew where Russell was coming from.

One time I got around Heinsohn and went in for a layup and Russell blocked it. Later I got around Heinsohn again,

went in for the layup and again Russell blocked it. The next
time I got around Heinsohn and went in for the layup, Russell
was nowhere near me, but I missed the shot because I was
looking for him.

The addition of Russell turned a good Boston team into a
great one. We made the playoffs that year and got into the
finals against the Celtics and lost the title. After the 1956-57
season, I returned home and started thinking of ways to improve my game. My shooting was good, I was learning moves
from the forward position and I had begun to rebound well,
but I was getting pushed around under the boards. My hands
were weak and it was easy to knock the ball away from me.

I had a close friend named Alvin Roy, who was the Olympic
weight lifting trainer at Helsinki in 1956. He had done a lot
of work with athletes like Billy Cannon and Jimmy Taylor, so
I asked him if there was anything he could do for me.

"Bob," he said, "of all the athletes I know, you are the one
I have not recommended weight training to because you have
been successful without it. But, since you asked, I can start
you on a program of weights which will help you with your
basketball. I won't put a lot of muscle on you. You'll gain only
four or five pounds a year, but I will make you stronger and
get you to the point where you will like contact under the
boards."

I started on Alvin's program and worked with weights three
times a week. Later, I worked on isometrics and the entire
weight program worked wonders for me. I am in favor of
working with weights, but never without strong supervision.

I reported to Concordia Seminary in St. Louis for the 1957-
58 season. Among the newcomers to the team were Win Wilfong, our first draft choice, and Walter Davis, the Olympic
high jumper, who came in a trade with Philadelphia. We had
a very powerful ball club. There was talent and spirit—a great
group of guys. At center we had Charlie Share, the forwards
were Cliff Hagen and myself, the guards were Slater Martin
and Jack McMahon and on the bench were Davis, Wilfong,

Med Park, Ed Macauley, and Jack Coleman. We fully expected to win the Western Division championship that year.

There was an unforgettable incident in St. Louis when Mc-Mahon got in a brawl with Detroit's George Yardley and I jumped right into the middle of it. I was trying to pull George off Jack and out of the corner of my eye I saw Joe Holup, who was 6′ 7″ and about 240 pounds. He took a running start from the sidelines and hit me with a body block and knocked me from mid-court all the way to the scorer's table.

The scorer's table in St. Louis has curtains hanging over the front and back and he knocked me under the curtains and I remember waking up and it was pitch dark and all I could think of was, "Oh, Lord, he has blinded me." I reached out, felt the curtain, raised it and peeked out and saw the fight was still going on, so I lowered the curtain and rested there until the police restored peace and quiet. I'd had enough for one fight.

We were winning the Western Division easily and I was leading the league in scoring. During Christmas week my mother and dad came up to see me play and during a game against Detroit, I got the ball at the backboard on a rebound and turned to come out and got sandwiched between Chuck Noble and George Yardley. Snap! I could hear my wrist crack and the pain was terrible. I came out with a broken metacarpal bone in my left hand. It was the second year in a row that I'd been knocked out of action when I was going well. My chance for the scoring crown disappeared again, so I concentrated on keeping myself in shape to help my team in the playoff.

At first I didn't play very much, then I started getting back into games and had my cast fixed again so when I raised my arm it was in shooting position. The ball club continued to do well without me. We won the Western Division championship by eight games and went into the playoffs. We went against the Minneapolis Lakers and we beat them and then we went against the Boston Celtics.

We played them the first two games in Boston. We won one

of the two and we won the first one at home but lost the second. Now we were tied at two games apiece. We went back to Boston for the next game and beat them. We were now leading three games to two and the sixth game was in St. Louis. If we won we would win the championship and if we lost we would have to go back to Boston for the seventh game and it was doubtful that we could beat them again up there. That sixth game was a great game, close all the way. I scored 50 points including 19 out of our last 21. I made a jump shot with about 15 seconds to go which put us ahead by three. They brought the ball in bounds, we let Bill Sharman walk in for a layup, which left us leading by one, 110 to 109. We threw the ball in bounds to Ed Macauley and the horn went off. Ed threw the ball high in the air. We had won the world championship!

To this day, Auerbach still needles Heinsohn that the Celtics would have won the championship that year too if Tommy had held me to 48 points.

Chapter 8 ● CLYDE AND LARRY ● After the 1958 season, I was invited to go on a basketball tour of the United States with a team made up of top NBA players. We were scheduled to play 21 games in 21 different cities in 22 nights.

It was on this tour that I became friendly with Clyde Lovellette and Larry Foust, who are two of the funniest men I have ever met. Individually, Clyde and Larry are funny; together, they are unbelievable.

I will never forget the night we played in Albuquerque, New Mexico. Larry and Clyde happened to be playing against one another and the game was going along when all of a sudden I heard the crowd roar and I looked up and there at mid-court Larry and Clyde were having a brawl.

They were carrying on and pushing and shoving and all of a sudden Lovellette pulled a pistol out of his trunks and shot Foust three times right there at mid-court and Larry went down. A woman screamed and people ran on the court.

This kind of shook the people up because they had never seen two men as big as Lovellette and Foust fighting, much less see someone get shot. Foust began writhing on the floor and Lovellette pointed the pistol at the crowd and fired! Caps! Only a cap pistol. Once they realized what had happened, the people just howled and howled, holding the game up for almost five minutes.

By a strange coincidence, both Lovellette and Foust wound up playing with us at the same time. Clyde came to us as center insurance in a five-player trade with Cincinnati before the

1958-59 season. Larry joined us in the middle of the following season and it seemed inevitable that the two should play on the same team. They complemented one another so well, they should have come as an entry.

Between the two of them, they kept us constantly in stitches with their antics and we were a very loose ball club while Clyde and Larry were there to carry on. They were funny men in different ways. Clyde's humor was spontaneous, while Larry was a planner. He would think up things to say and things to do.

When he joined us, Lovellette moved into the George Washington Hotel, where I was living. He was a fanatic for guns and h‿ got a lot of publicity around the country for being a quick draw. I never saw him draw, and frankly, I doubt if all the publicity was justified. But he played the game very well. He would walk around the hotel with his blue denim coat, ten-gallon hat, cowboy boots and six-guns loaded with blanks. One day he was practicing his draw and he shot himself in the leg with a blank.

Whenever we played at home on Tuesday nights, you could always depend on Clyde arriving late for the game. There was a fellow named Chris Colt, who had a cowboy show in St. Louis every Tuesday night and he lived in our hotel. Clyde would wait until Christ Colt got home from his show and the two of them would draw against one another in the middle of the street, like in the picture "High Noon." Clyde swore he never lost a "gun battle" with Chris Colt.

The thing I remember most about Clyde is he took his guns with him on one trip and during one game, Clyde felt he was getting a hard time from this one official, Jim Duffy of Providence, Rhode Island. Jim was the most likable guy in the world but he had an Irish temper. There was a big argument and Duffy threw Lovellette out of the game.

Clyde was so upset, he waited for Duffy outside the auditorium after the game and when Jim came by, Clyde said, "Duffy, you so and so, you threw me out of that ball game."

"Yes," Duffy said calmly, "and I will do it again if you say something to me that I don't like."

"You do that again and I'll kill you," Lovellette shouted. "In fact, I'm going to kill you anyway. I'm sick of you picking on me all the time."

Whereupon Clyde went back to his room, put on his guns loaded with blanks, and waited for Duffy to arrive at his hotel floor.

When Jim got off the elevator, Clyde leaped from behind a door, pulled out his six-shooter loaded with blanks and fired four shots at Duffy from eight feet away. "I told you I'd kill you," he hollered. Poor Jim almost keeled over from fright and Clyde just stood there and laughed.

Occasionally Clyde was on the other end. One season Clyde was fined $75 because three times in a row he didn't get back on defense. In his contract for the next year, Clyde said he was going to ask Mr. Kerner for three no-get-backers a month.

Larry Foust came along later and immediately began competing with Lovellette for laughs. The result for us was one hilarious moment after another.

Larry considered himself an expert golfer and one time I was playing in a foursome with him and he was on the third tee. He approached the ball and took a tremendous swing and barely tipped the ball. It skidded off his driver about fifteen feet and landed right in his golf cart, which was off to the side.

So Larry immediately jumped into the cart, drove to the green, kicked his ball out five inches from the cup, sank it and claimed a double eagle.

Once we were in Los Angeles waiting to play the Lakers and it was about 5:30 in the afternoon, so I went up to take a nap. After I left, Larry went up to his room, took off all his clothes and put a towel around him like a loin cloth. Then he went to the closet and got a metal clothes hanger and unraveled it. He got his shaving cream and put it all over his face and on top of the shaving cream he put corn flakes; then he came to my room and knocked on the door.

"Who is it? Who is it?" I kept screaming, because I had dozed off and I was annoyed that someone was disturbing my rest. When there was no answer, I stumbled out of bed and opened the door. The room was all dark and I was half asleep and when I opened the door this thing dashed into the room, screaming and jumping up and down and I almost fainted because at first I didn't know who it was. Larry fell on the floor and practically killed himself laughing.

One night we were playing a big game in Philadelphia. Paul Seymour was our coach at the time and he liked to give us pep talks before big games.

"Fellows," he said, "this is a very big game. We need this one badly, but we can do it. We can beat them."

It was a very important game and we were so fired up, we were practically ready to run through the wall and just as we were about to leave, Larry Foust raised his hand.

"What do you want, Foust?" Paul asked.

"Paul," Larry said with a quizzical expression on his face, "do you honestly think we have a chance to win this game tonight?"

Larry and Clyde were nearing the end of their fine careers and I knew this couldn't go on forever. Just the same it was a shock when Lovellette was traded to Boston just before the 1962-63 season. It was a sad day when Clyde left and equally sad when Larry retired. When they left our club, it was the end of something special for me.

Chapter 9 ● **THE GOOD YEARS** ● We reached the top of the world in 1958. As NBA champions, we became national celebrities and we all gloried in the attention and adulations which followed. There were banquets and endorsements and exhibition tours and many of us made money over and above the winning playoff share.

Personally, it was the peak of my professional career. I felt I had really arrived as a professional basketball player and I was anxiously looking forward to the future.

The following year we had practically the same team back and it was expected we would have another great team and be in contention to repeat as world champions.

We had a good year, winning the Western Division with a record of 49-23. In the East, Boston won easily. I averaged 29.2 points a game and set an NBA scoring record with 2,105 points. The year before George Yardley had scored 2,001 points to become the first player to score over 2,000 points in a season. I dropped out of contention for the scoring championship that year because of my broken hand, but in 1958-59, I not only beat Yardley's record, I also broke the all-time average per game scoring record of 28.5, which had been held by George Mikan. Twice that year I hit 50 points or more—52 against Boston and 50 against Detroit.

We added Si Green in the middle of the season in a trade with Cincinnati for Med Park, who had been my roommate, running mate, and close friend for four years. I hated to see

Med leave, but in Si Green, we got a three-time All-America from Duquesne and a fine professional player.

I owe Si whatever ability I have as a driver. One day at practice, noticing that I was having difficulty going past my defensive man, Si took me aside and gave me some tips I put to immediate good use.

He pointed out that the secret is in the first step. In driving to my left side, for example, Si demonstrated how my first step should be with my right foot and as close to the side of the foot of my defensive man and as far behind him as possible.

Driving to the right, the long first step should be made with the left foot.

The ball is shielded on the far side of the driver's body away from the defensive man and as the forward move is made, the ball is put out in front, setting up dribbling momentum toward the basket.

Si's advice about that important first step while protecting the ball proved to be invaluable.

In the playoffs, we went to Minneapolis and were beaten by the Lakers in six games, which was a great disappointment to all of us. It was the first time we had not gone into the finals against the Celtics. Boston beat the Lakers in four straight. The Celtics have been champions every year I played after that.

At the beginning of the 1959-60 season, Marty Blake set up some exhibition games on the West Coast, which still didn't have professional basketball. We played in Los Angeles, San Francisco, Las Vegas, Albuquerque and Lubbock, Texas.

We were in Los Angeles for three days and I happened to have a friend, Guy McElwayne, who worked for M-G-M. Guy took me and a few of the boys to the studio where they were making a movie with Ernest Borgnine, Anthony Franciosa and Gina Lollobrigida. He arranged for me to pose for pictures with Miss Lollobrigida.

It happened it was after a scene in which she wore a negligee. We were under these hot lights and I had on a warm sports coat. Gina was very nice and I thought she was the loveliest thing I had ever seen. She took me by the arm and I was looking at her, perspiration dripping down my forehead, and trying to be suave. This was my big chance to be a smooth talker. I was a big man from the East and I was going to make a big impression on her. She was very polite, although she had never heard of me and could have cared less. This was just part of her job.

"You play basketball, don't you?" she asked.

This was my big chance. "Yup," I said.

"Do you play with the Globetrotters?"

"Nope."

"Are you married?"

"Nope."

That was the entire conversation. My big opportunity, my big chance with Gina Lollobrigida and all I could say were two "nopes" and a "yup." I couldn't understand why she didn't flip for me. It always worked for Gary Cooper.

We bounced back from being eliminated in the playoffs the year before. Charlie Share had been traded to Minneapolis and our new starting center was Clyde Lovellette. We had the highest scoring front line in history, with me at one forward (26.1 points per game), Cliff Hagan at the other forward (24.8) and Lovellette (20.8) at center.

We finished with a record of 46-29 and beat Minneapolis in seven games for the Western title. Then we went to play the Boston Celtics and they beat us in seven games.

I had a good year in the 1960-61 season. I averaged 27.9 points per game and I was fourth in the league in scoring and had my best rebounding year with 20.3 rebounds per game, third in the league.

Our first draft choice that year was Lenny Wilkins, who came to us from Providence College. We had heard a lot about him and he came into training camp and had a tough time at first. We had two fine rookie guards and there was just one spot open. So it was narrowed down to Wilkins and Rollie

1

With the exception of Elgin Baylor, Cliff Hagan of the Hawks has the greatest variety of offensive moves in basketball. Equally adept with a hook (1), a jumper (2), or a drive (3), Cliff compensated for his lack of height (6'4") with tremendous jumping ability and great hands.

2

For a big man (6′9″) Clyde Lovellette had the best touch I've ever seen. He was as accurate with a one hand set (1) as any player in the game. His hook was equally as effective and Clyde was one of the top ten scorers in NBA history.

Stevens. I knew it was going to be a tough decision, but Paul Seymour decided Wilkins had more potential. It turned out to be a tremendous decision because Lenny has become one of the outstanding guards in professional basketball.

Lenny came into the league the same year as Oscar Robertson and Jerry West. Oscar averaged over 30 points a game as a rookie and Jerry averaged about 17.5. These two young men, along with Bob Cousy, rank in my book as the outstanding guards of all time.

Med Park had been in Cincinnati the previous year and before we had ever seen Robertson play, Med told me Oscar was a great passer and playmaker, but he couldn't hit a 15-foot jump shot. In training camp he hadn't been shooting well and Med said you could lay off Oscar and you wouldn't have to worry about him hitting that shot. Well, Med Park will never live this down because Oscar has proved he can shoot from any distance.

When we started playing Oscar we dropped off him and let him shoot because of Med's report, but we quickly learned our error.

After our exhibition series we played several games with Cincinnati and Oscar was a super ball player and everybody on the team realized it. All the writers came around and asked us what we thought of him. Everybody had nothing but praise, but Larry Foust, being the comedian he is, figured he would shake the writers.

"He'll never make it," Larry said, and it was printed all over the country.

The summer before, the Minneapolis Lakers had moved to Los Angeles after much resistance from owners and coaches in the league. They didn't want Minneapolis to move to Los Angeles because it was too far to travel. They would agree to the switch if another team moved to the West Coast with them, but it didn't work out and the Lakers were finally given permission to move alone. Eventually, San Francisco also had a franchise.

The Lakers had a fine playoff against us. We went to seven

games and the sixth was an unbelievable game, it was so close. We had about 35 seconds to play and Los Angeles had the ball and we were five points down. They took a shot and missed and we came down and made a three-point play, which cut their lead to two with 10 seconds left. Los Angeles took the ball, threw it in bounds and one of their guards tried to pass to another guard and the ball went out of bounds. Now there were five seconds left and we had the ball, two points down. We threw the ball in to Lenny Wilkins who dribbled the length of the court and was fouled in the act of shooting. With two seconds to go, Lenny had two free throws. The pressure was unbelievable. There were over 14,000 people there and Lenny Wilkins stood at the free throw line with the crowd screaming at him as loud as it could and made both free throws. Right then I knew he was going to be a great professional. Lenny tied the game and we beat them in overtime, 114-113.

Despite the Lakers' defeat, everybody in Los Angeles said this one game made professional basketball on the West Coast. Los Angeles had been very big on baseball and pro football, but they had never seen pro basketball and after this game a lot of people in Los Angeles bought season tickets to the Lakers' games for the next season and the Lakers made their franchise on the West Coast. They became a most success-ful franchise in basketball and this one game had more to do with it than anything else. We went back to St. Louis for the seventh game and beat Los Angeles, 105-103, for the Western title, but the Celtics beat us in five games. It was getting mo-notonous.

In 1961-62, we had the same team except for Lenny Wilkins who had gone into the service. His absence left a huge gap at guard and it was the worst year we ever had in St. Louis. Our record was 29 and 51, the first losing season we ever had in St. Louis. Ironically, it was the only time I averaged over 30 points per game. I averaged 31.1 points and 18.7 rebounds, but it meant nothing because of the other things that hap-pened.

Everything went wrong. Lenny Wilkins played only 15 or

20 games because he was stationed in Washington, D.C. and flew in for our weekend games. Clyde Lovellette and Larry Foust both got hurt and played about half the season. Mr. Kerner brought in players from all over the United States, out of the Eastern League, out of other professional basketball teams. We had a total of 18 different players on our roster one time or another during this season.

Several things happened that year that are worth mentioning. One was Elgin Baylor's averaging 38.2 points per game. This is the greatest scoring I have ever seen by any player in professional basketball. Others have averaged more, but for a man only 6' 5" averaging 38.2 points per game is an unbelievable feat. He didn't win the scoring championship because Wilt Chamberlain had averaged about 50 points that year, but Elgin's was, to me, an unbelievable performance.

The 1962-63 season was the year Mr. Kerner did his tremendous job of reorganizing the entire team. He started the season with nine players who were not there the year before and only Cliff Hagan and myself were held over. That was also the year Harry Gallatin took over as coach.

Our first draft choice was Zelmo Beaty. When we first heard the name we kidded Zelmo and said it sounded more like a soft drink or a circus performer than a basketball player, but he was quite a ball player.

The year before, when we were so horrible, was the year the American Basketball League was founded. They had quite a few professional players and some college boys and one of our old players, Jack McMahon was the coach of the Kansas City Steers. Mr. Kerner and Marty Blake started scouting the ABL and trading around our league for the rights to a lot of these players. They worked out a deal for the rights to Mike Farmer, who was with San Francisco. They worked out a deal with Chicago for the rights to Bill Bridges, the leading scorer in the ABL. Gene Tormehlen was owned by us but played in that league. Somehow Mr. Kerner got the rights to John Barnhill. Our fourth draft choice was a boy from Southern Illinois named Charlie Vaughn and a lot of people couldn't understand how he had been selected on the fourth round because he has as much talent as any guard in professional basketball.

Phil Jordan came with us and did a tremendous job at center while Zelmo Beatty was learning. For the first 15 of 20 games, Phil was the starting center and then Zelmo came in. I enjoyed Phil Jordan quite a bit. He and Barney Cable had an apartment together over Gaslight Square in St. Louis and Phil was quite a guitar player and singer and I have always loved country music. So Phil, Barney, Gene Tormehlen and I would go to Phil's apartment and he would pull out that guitar and start singing and we had an old-fashioned hillbilly session!

The team did well. Mike Farmer did an especially good job. He became one of the best defensive forwards in basketball. He is a sound, steady ball player who scores 12 or 14 points a game, shoots about 50 percent from the floor and 85-90 percent at the foul line, never makes a mistake and gives you great defense.

In the playoffs we beat Detroit in four games. I averaged about 38 points per game against Detroit. We went to play Los Angeles and, as usual, we had a terrific series against them and they beat us in the seventh game in Los Angeles. Actually, we really lost in the second game. We lost the first game, but in the second game we had them down seven points with one minute and 50 seconds to go and we lost the game. They beat us by two. Jerry West made a basket as the gun went off to beat us. The Celtics beat the Lakers in six for the NBA title.

In the 1963-64 season Richie Guerin was added to our ball club in November. Mr. Kerner bought him from the New York Knickerbockers. Richie was a tremendous addition. We now had Wilkins, Barnhill, Vaughn and Richie in our back court. Richie had a reputation in New York for being a gunner, but he is a real sound basketball player and a good passer and I enjoyed playing with him. He was a big help to me all season.

Going into the last game of the season we were one game behind San Francisco and it could easily have ended in a tie but we played in Detroit and were beaten.

San Francisco won the regular season and in the playoffs we

beat Los Angeles and went against the Warriors. They had Wilt Chamberlain, Nate Thurmond at forward, Tom Meschery, Guy Rogers and Gary Phillips. Thurmond played me that year and he is about 6' 11" and strong as an ox. He is going to be one of the super stars of the future. With Wilt and Thurmond in the front line we didn't come close to getting a rebound. They beat us in the seventh game in San Francisco. Again, the Western division representative lost to the Celtics, this time in five games.

Chapter 10 ● ABROAD ● Sometime during the 1963 season, Red Auerbach, coach of the Boston Celtics, mentioned something about a basketball tour the State Department had asked him to head up. Red would be in charge of a team of All-Stars and they would go to Communist countries to play, teach and lecture on basketball. There was a good chance, the State Department said, that Russia would be included in the trip.

Red asked me if I would be interested in such a trip and I said certainly because I knew it was an opportunity of a lifetime. The tour was arranged and on May 1, 1964, we all met in Washington, D.C. for briefing by the State Department. There was Bob Cousy, Oscar Robertson, K.C. Jones, Tom Gola, Jerry Lucas, Tom Heinsohn, Bill Russell and myself, plus Red and the Celtics' trainer, Buddy LeRoux.

We were briefed for two days and afterwards we were taken to the White House to meet President Johnson, which was quite a thrill. He shook hands with each of us and wished us luck on the trip. And we took a group picture with the President.

During the briefings, they broke down each country we were to visit and told us how to act and what to expect. Russell fell asleep during Poland and began snoring during Yugoslavia. They told us of the atrocities committed against the Poles and how much they hated Germans and Heinsohn asked if he could change his name to O'Shea. Among the things we were told was not to take it easy on any of the teams we played.

At the last minute we discovered we would not be permitted

to go to Russia. The State Department was disappointed and so were we.

First stop was Warsaw, Poland. The people were friendly and they seemed sincerely interested in the United States. We had a wonderful time there and played in four cities—Warsaw, Gdansk, Krakow and Wroclaw.

I roomed with Bob Cousy for the six week trip. In these countries they did not have many of the luxuries of life— toilet tissue was like sand paper. I happened to bring four rolls of good, old American toilet paper and the greatest sign of friendship I could show Cousy was to share it with him. I hope he realizes I saved his life.

The first night we played in a very old arena. It seated about 4,500 and the game had been sold out for months. Around the arena they had about 200 soldiers with burp guns standing there looking for gate crashers, they said, but I wasn't so sure and I was a little nervous.

We spent a day visiting the concentration camp at Auschwitz. Of all the places I have ever been, this left the most vivid impression on me. The Poles have made the Auschwitz camp a national shrine. They don't let the people forget how the Nazis treated them. They turned the barracks into rooms with glass fronts and you can look right into them. One room is piled with hair from prisoners, another with spectacles, another with old clothes and it got to the point where it made you sick to look at all this.

We spent the whole day looking and taking pictures. In a semi-buried building we saw the rooms where the Nazis would strip prisoners naked and tell them they were going to give them a shower. Instead they would lock them in and instead of water, they would pipe in poison gas which killed them. Then they would take the bodies next door and burn them by the thousands in ovens.

Seeing these things shakes you up and makes you thank God for being brought up in a country like the United States, with all its wonderful opportunities and advantages.

Tom Heinsohn has a German-sounding name and he is tall

with blue eyes and a blond crew cut and he was very nervous the whole time we were in Poland. At the games we would step forward as our names were called and you could hear this murmur go through the crowd when Tom Heinsohn was introduced. We would all holler "Kraut" and "Deutsch" as he stood out there and this would agitate the crowd.

Tommy is usually very sociable. He likes to go out and sit around and talk to people, but when we were in Poland he didn't leave his hotel room very much. So Red and Cousy had this idea. They got two high school coaches to dress up like the secret police with trench coats and big hats and make believe they were going to arrest Tommy. This was mostly Red's idea. He was getting revenge because the year before Tommy had given Red an exploding cigar. We all went back to the hotel and hid and watched. The two men came up and knocked at Heinsohn's door and Tommy answered it. One guy had a basketball medal pinned to the inside of his trench coat and he flashed it and said, "Police. You Heinsohn?"

Tommy said, "Uh-huh."

"Get your passport," the man said. "You are under arrest."

Tommy nearly died because he had been imagining this would happen to him. Lucas, Gola and Heinsohn were rooming together and Lucas was lying on the bed and he jumped up to see what was happening. Gola was shaving and Heinsohn turned to him. "Tom, they are taking me away."

Heinsohn got dressed and one guy stood in front of him and the other stood in back of him with his finger in his pocket like he was carrying a gun and he stuck it in Heinsohn's back. Gola never stopped shaving and Lucas just stood there watching pop-eyed as they marched Heinsohn out the door.

"Get Auerbach," Heinsohn said frantically. "Tell him to come and get me out of this."

"Cool it, dad," Gola said, never missing a stroke. "I'll handle it, don't worry."

They marched Heinsohn out of the room, down the stairs, into the street and down about a half block to a restaurant.

"Wait here," they said. "We are going to get the car. We will be right back."

And they left him and Tommy just sat there like the world was coming to an end. He never moved. About twenty minutes later, we all walked into the restaurant and Heinsohn took one look at our faces and he knew what we had done. He vowed revenge on everyone present but he was a good sport about it . . . he didn't kill Red.

One night Bob Cousy and I were walking around Krakow and we came to a square where a celebration was going on. We looked up the street and saw a man being tossed into the air about 15 feet and when he could come down, they would toss him back up and all the time he was hollering for help. We moved closer and saw about ten students had Auerbach and they were throwing him in the air. We were on the other side of the street just watching and killing ourselves laughing and Auerbach looked over at us and said, "That tall one, get him."

About 15 students started coming after me and I didn't know whether to run or laugh, so I just stood there like a big jerk. Cousy ran. They grabbed me and started throwing me in the air and the only thing I could think of doing was put one hand on my passport and the other hand on my wallet. They could break my neck, but I wasn't going to lose my passport or my wallet.

We traveled in Poland, Egypt, Romania and Yugoslavia. We played mostly outdoor games and just about everywhere we went we received a tremendous reception. In Egypt, every door was open to us and we were treated like kings.

I remember we had a General Tados who was assigned to take us all over. He and his wife traveled with us and were just as nice as they could be. We got in with the American Embassy people to see the governor of Cairo and were told it was the first time the American Embassy people had been able to see him in two years.

One day we were standing on a street corner in Alexandria, just looking out at the Mediterranean, when we heard sirens screaming and we looked up and saw a big black limousine with about 30 motorcycle policemen. There was Nikita Khrushchev in the back seat going to Cairo after visiting Nasser.

The most memorable incident happened in Yugoslavia. We were playing the first night in Belgrade in an outdoor arena before 15,000 people. When we walked out on the court we sensed a strange atmosphere. Everywhere else the people realized what a great basketball team we were. They had heard about us and we were billed as the greatest basketball team in the world everywhere we went. And we were the greatest basketball team ever assembled, without a doubt. During this tour we played 22 games and won all 22 of them by 20 to 60 points.

But in Yugoslavia we realized these people were there to beat our brains out, not to admire our basketball. These were the roughest games I have ever played in.

The first time down the court there was a center jump and Russell got the tip. He threw the ball to Heinsohn, who took one of his hook shots and a guy punched him in the stomach and flattened him right on the court. Tommy jumped up and was holding his stomach and running after this guy and he got him about three-fourths of the way down the court and Tommy hit him with a forearm and knocked him into the second row of bleachers. This started it.

The next time down the court a guy tripped Russell and he sprawled over the court and he got up without saying a word. The same thing happened a second time and Bill didn't say a thing. The next time they threw the ball to him he turned and led with an elbow and hit the guy that had tripped him right on the point of the jaw and they carried this guy off the court. It was so rough that when you went up for a layup you didn't watch the basket. You shot with your right hand and punched with your left. We thought we were going to be killed by the mob after the game. We won by about 25 points but it was so rough you just couldn't imagine it.

We went to another town and it was exactly the same. There were about 15,000 people screaming at us. We made up our minds to give it to them with all we had. We beat them by 58 points. I will never forget Russell blocking almost every shot they took. They couldn't get the ball even two feet in the air.

When the shoving and mauling got completely out of hand late in the game, we changed tactics, using embarrassment as a weapon instead of fists.

Cooz started dribbling behind his back and shooting from behind, not even looking at the basket. I got up to the foul line to shoot and put one up with my back to the hoop.

With seconds to go, Oscar Robertson brought the ball from back to front court with his defensive man draped over his shoulders, clawing and pummeling Oscar to get the ball. Just before the final horn, the Big O wrenched free, and then with a smile, handed the ball to his surprised guard, and walked away.

The game ended with this fellow just standing there in disbelief, staring at the ball in his hands.

People ask, "How come you got rough with these people when you are on a good will tour for the United States?" But we figured the people in Yugoslavia were tough and the worst thing we could do on this tour was to let them push us around. We had to fight back and we did just that on the basketball court.

Except for those two towns in Yugoslavia, it was an interesting and enjoyable experience.

We were surprised that most teams were as good as they were. Even though we beat them badly they still had good teams. They took films of every game we played, every scrimmage we had and every clinic we held and these films will be shipped to all the Communist countries and pretty soon you will be seeing guys going behind their backs like Cousy and dribbling like Oscar and blocking shots like Russell.

When the tour was over Tom Gola, K.C. Jones and I went to Rome for three days. K.C. was going on to Africa to give clinics for the State Department. Gola and I went to the Riviera after Rome and stayed there four days to get some sun and to rest. Then we came back to the United States.

Chapter 11 ● COACHES, COACHES AND MORE COACHES ● I have played for quite an assortment of coaches since I turned pro—nine of them in eleven years—and I have been asked which was the greatest coach I ever played for. I find it impossible to answer that question. Each of them had his good points and each had his failings and of the nine, no two were alike.

They ranged from the hard-nosed Alex Hannum to the nice-guy Fuzzy Levane and I can honestly say I never had any trouble with any of them. Each had something to do with my career and each will remain memorable for one thing or another.

Although I took a brief fling at running the club as an interim coach, I never seriously considered becoming a coach in the pros. When I was through playing, I wanted to enter the business world.

The most important thing a coach must have is the ability to handle players and I don't think you acquire this. I think this is innate. It is important, for instance, for a coach to handle the situation correctly when a player makes a big mistake that costs a game. No two players can be handled in the same manner.

I have never approved of a coach chewing a player out in front of the whole team. I believe he should take the player aside and tell him what he did wrong. That is a general view because personally I didn't mind being chewed out in front of the entire team since we are all working out there together and they knew, as well as I did, that I made a mistake.

One thing I feel strongly about is that it not get out to the papers when a player is reprimanded. What goes on in the locker room should stay in the locker room.

I suppose when I think of my coaches, the one I will think of first is Red Holzman and that is only natural because he was my first professional coach. I went to him when I was green and impressionable and he seemed so experienced and wise to me. One thing for which I will always be indebted to Red is switching me from center to forward.

Red was a great one for meetings. In my rookie year we were terrible and Red worried a lot about his job. About every two weeks, he would call us together for a meeting in his hotel room. He would tell us what we were doing wrong and then he would ask for our opinions on what we thought was wrong with the team.

We all had our own ideas, but none of us ever put the blame on ourselves. Inevitably, as the meeting ended, Red would reach into his wallet and pull out a picture of his six-year-old daughter.

"Fellows," he would say, "here is a picture of my daughter. She is as pretty as a picture and I love her very much. But she likes to eat and if you guys keep losing I am going to lose my job and I will not have enough money to buy food for my daughter and she will go hungry. So, for goodness sakes, win for my daughter."

Red was finally let go in the 1956-57 season and Mr. Kerner decided the man he wanted to coach the team was Slater Martin, who had joined us a month earlier in a trade designed to bolster our guard position. Slater gave it a try, but after two games he went to Mr. Kerner.

"I have enough trouble just playing, Mr. Kerner. I can't coach. It's driving me crazy."

"I understand, Slater," Mr. Kerner said.

Alex Hannum was a second stringer on the team and Mr. Kerner picked him to succeed Martin, but he made one request of Slater.

"Stay as coach in name only," he asked. "For six more games. Hannum will handle the club, but how will it look if I replace you after only two games?"

So Alex Hannum was named coach after Martin was in charge for eight games, according to the books, and it was a great break for Alex because he went on to become one of the top coaches in the game. The following year, he led us to the World Championship, the first time St. Louis had won the title and the last time Boston lost it.

After we won the title, Mr. Kerner and Hannum had a dispute over contracts. I don't believe money was the issue, I think it was length of contract. They couldn't get together and even though the Hawks were World Champions, Alex was not rehired as coach—exactly the same situation that happened in St. Louis in baseball with Johnny Keane after the 1964 season.

As Hannum's replacement Mr. Kerner selected Andy Phillip, who had been a great player for Fort Wayne and had finished up a fine career with the Celtics.

Andy was the first coach I ever played for who went in strongly for calisthenics and drills. He started the season with us and after 10 games, Mr. Kerner decided on a change. We had won 6 of 10 but Mr. Kerner just didn't like the way Andy handled things and he decided to get rid of him before things got out of hand. He didn't think Andy was getting the most out of his players, so one day he called in Ed Macauley.

"Ed," he said, "I'm going to play Russian Roulette with you. I can do one of three things: I can trade you, you can retire, or, you can become coach of the St. Louis Hawks."

Ed Macauley was a very astute coach. He wasn't a shouter or a hollerer. He would sit down and reason things out with his players when something went wrong. We won the division championship by 15 games, but we were upset in the playoffs by the Lakers in five games and I still maintain the reason we lost was that Slater Martin had been injured late in the season and was unable to play at all in the playoffs.

The following year we won by 16 games with Macauley as coach and we made it to the finals, only to lose to Boston in seven games.

I was in Baton Rouge during the summer of 1960, when I learned Ed Macauley would not be our coach for the 1960-61 season. He was promoted to general manager and Paul Seymour was given a three-year contract to take over. Paul had been the coach at Syracuse, where he had an outstanding record and he was generally conceded to be one of the brightest young coaches in the business.

I regret to say it was while Paul Seymour was coaching that I had the most unfortunate incident of my professional career. During all the years I played pro ball, I was always conscious of the image I presented to the public. Only once have I ever had something said about me which was detrimental to my character and I feel I should explain exactly what happened.

It was in 1961, the second year of Seymour's three-year contract, and our first draft choice—handpicked by Seymour— was a boy named Cleo Hill of Winston-Salem College.

We had practically an all-veteran team in camp that year. Our front line consisted of Clyde Lovellette, Cliff Hagan and myself and the backcourt had Johnny McCarthy, Al Ferrari and Si Green.

Seymour began pushing Hill from the first day of camp. He would say to some guard—Ferrari, for instance—"Watch how Cleo dribbles and you might learn something."

This made Al so mad, he was ready to tear the place down because he was fighting for his job and he was a good basketball player and a tremendous competitor.

Then Seymour might go to another guard and say, "John, that Hill can shoot. You can learn something from him."

This made our guards mad because Cleo was practically handed a starting job right from opening day of camp. During the season Lovellette and Larry Foust got hurt and everything started going to pot and we just kept losing. Paul was still pushing Cleo and that was doing our morale no good, so one night I went to him in confidence.

"Paul, this may be none of my business, but I am captain of the team and I'd like to get this off my chest. I feel if you leave Cleo alone and don't push him so much, he will work his way into our lineup and be a big help to us before the year is out. I think he is being pushed too fast and the others—particularly the guards—resent it."

"Bob," Paul said, "you're probably right. I never thought of it that way. I certainly never meant to do it that way. I will try another way and see what happens."

That was the last I heard of that until we went into Detroit and Paul told the press he would trade any of his ball players, with no exception. It was inevitable now that he would clash with Mr. Kerner.

Later on, I heard Paul had been fired, but I didn't know too much about it. The next day I picked up the paper and read his statement. The reason he had been fired, he said, was that he was taking up for Cleo Hill and some of the veteran players resented it. He said he wouldn't dream of treating a dog the way Pettit, Lovellette and Hagan treated Cleo.

I have played with many ball players, and I think I would know if my teammates or I were treating a man unfairly. I never treated Cleo or anyone except the way I'd expect to be treated myself, and I can say the same for Cliff and Clyde. We all were pulling for Cleo because we were going so bad. I would have loved to see him become another Bob Cousy or Oscar Robertson and make us a much better team. Heaven knows, we could have used a player of that caliber.

Paul also said one of his veteran players had complained that Cleo was getting too many headlines. Naturally, he meant me. But I couldn't care less how many headlines Cleo Hill got because I have had enough in eleven years to last ten people a lifetime. Headlines made no difference to me. I had gone to Seymour for the good of the club, and in confidence, and everything had been turned around.

Nothing could have hurt me more. I got letters from all over the country, people saying, "Bob Pettit, you may be a great basketball player, but your character stinks."

I made headlines around the country because it seemed that I, as a Southerner, was unable to get along with a Negro teammate. This hurt because I have never had anything but good relations with boys I played with or against. I don't care what race a man is or what color his skin is—all I care about is can he play basketball.

After Seymour was fired, Mr. Kerner hired Fuzzy Levane, who had been the successful coach of the New York Knicks and who had coached the Hawks in Milwaukee before I joined the club. I don't think I ever enjoyed playing for someone as much as Fuzzy Levane. He is a jewel of a man. He was so easy to get along with and so funny, we were all crazy about him. All the players wanted to play so hard for him, but we just didn't have it that year. We couldn't do a thing right.

One night in New York, a newspaperman questioned Fuzzy's strategy. "Coach," he said, "do you mind explaining a couple of moves?"

"Listen, sport," Fuzzy said, "don't call me coach, I'm no coach, I am a zoo keeper."

Another time a reporter asked, "Fuzzy, what do you need more than anything else for this club?"

"More than anything else," Fuzzy said, "we need three psychiatrists and a baby-sitter."

Two of the players on the team were Bobby Simms and Shelley McMillan. Shelley was supposed to pick Bobby up one morning to go to the airport. He forgot to pick him up so Bobby had to catch a cab. Bobby asked Shelley why he didn't pick him up and they got into a violent argument in the lobby of the airport. Soon it developed into a fist fight and they were rolling on the floor and knocking down chairs and people started screaming from everywhere. Fuzzy was sitting in a chair right near the fight and they both rolled under his feet and Fuzzy never quit reading his paper the whole time. He just raised his feet up while Bobby and Shelley continued to fight.

For the 1962-63 season, Mr. Kerner cleaned house and when his broom swept, it took Fuzzy right with it. He not only got nine new ballplayers, the first thing he did was hire Harry Gallatin as coach. Harry had been a tremendous player for New York and Detroit and for three years he was a successful coach at Southern Illinois University.

Mr. Kerner actually hired Harry at the end of the previous season so he could go out and scout the colleges for potential draftees.

Gallatin did one of the best coaching jobs I have ever seen and Mr. Kerner did a fantastic job of providing him with players. Harry changed our offense all around. The Hawks had always been a running team, but Harry made us slow down and practice ball control. Some players objected and I was one of them because I always liked to run and shoot, but I went along with Harry and you certainly couldn't argue with the results. He took a team that was 29-51 the year before and turned it into a 48-32 team.

Another drastic thing Gallatin did was put Cliff Hagan on the bench for the first time and start Mike Farmer in his place. He made Hagan a fireman. He would have Cliff come off the bench and play the same role Frank Ramsey and then John Havlicek played in Boston. Cliff averaged 18 points a game in his new job, though he played only about 20 minutes a game. I know it hurt his pride not to start, but this is the way Gallatin wanted it and you have to admire his courage because Hagan is one of the most popular players ever to play in St. Louis.

Harry got us into the playoffs and he was voted the Coach of the Year in the NBA, an honor that was richly deserved. Gallatin coached through the 1963-64 season but the next season we were going badly and it was inevitable Harry would go.

Harry was replaced by another former Knickerbocker, Richie Guerin, who had joined us the previous year. So, Richie was the last coach I ever played for and the one thing I can tell about Richie is that he has the knack of handling players just as Alex Hannum had it. He gets the most out of everyone who plays for him and I predict Richie Guerin will develop into one of the best coaches in pro basketball.

Chapter 12 ● THE CELTICS ● In any era, any sport, one team dominates. Take the Yankees in baseball, the Cleveland Browns in football, Notre Dame in college football, Montreal in hockey. But no team has ever dominated a sport like the Boston Celtics in professional basketball.

Through 1965, they have won seven straight championships and eight of the last nine. We happened to be the last team to beat them for the championship and that was way back in 1958. Since then they have won everything—to play during their tremendous streak can get to be very frustrating, let me tell you.

Still, you cannot help but admire the Celtics. They are, without a doubt, the greatest basketball team ever assembled anytime, anywhere. Through the years they have had great guards like Bob Cousy, Bill Sharman, Frank Ramsey, K.C. Jones and Sam Jones; great forwards like Tommy Heinsohn, Jim Loscutoff, Tom Sanders and John Havlicek; tremendous centers like Ed Macauley; and the greatest player in the world, Bill Russell.

Red Auerbach has had a lot to do with their success. He is the greatest coach in basketball. His record certainly bears that out without a doubt. A coach has to be the absolute boss of a club. He must rule with an iron hand and Red does just that. He knows basketball and he has the rare ability of getting a team "up" for a game. Any time his team comes into the huddle, he has a play that helps get them out of trouble. Players respect this in a coach; they know they can fall back on someone when things aren't going right. Red also knows how to handle a team on substitutions. He knows just when to replace a man.

Of course, he has Bill Russell and that alone would help any man become a good coach. A lot of people still poke fun at the Hawks for letting Russell get away back in 1956. But I still maintain that St. Louis did the right thing. We were struggling for our lives and we needed immediate help; Ed Macauley and Cliff Hagan gave it to us. Ed brought immediate help at the gate because he was such a favorite in St. Louis, having played for St. Louis University. If we had had to wait for Russell to come along we might not have made it and the team might have folded.

However, you must also credit Auerbach's magnificent eye for talent. He recognized in Russell abilities that hadn't shown themselves in college and he gave up two top players merely for the chance to sign Bill. That decision made Red and it made the Celtics.

I have been asked many times which team would win if the Celtics of today played the Celtics of a half dozen years ago. I would have to pick the current team because of defense. The old Celtics had more scoring punch with Cousy and Sharman in back court, but this team today kills you with speed and defense.

K.C. Jones is probably the best defensive guard who ever played the game. He and Sam Jones are so great at stealing the ball; they put pressure on a team at mid-court and you never get a chance to develop your offensive patterns.

Sanders is the best defensive forward in basketball and, of course, there is Russell, who is a better player now than he was six years ago and that is gilding the lily because he was great then, too.

This team may not shoot as well but it can upset and distract a team with speed and defense. And good defense is still the best offense.

Defense, to me, has always been a matter of pride and the Celtics take pride in their great defense. Pride is essential because the glory goes to the scorers and nothing you do on defense shows up in the box score. But no high school, college or pro player fails to have a feeling of pride when he picks up the newspaper the day after the game and sees he held the man he was guarding well below his average.

No team has more confidence than one which can play defense because that team knows it can win even when it is not shooting well. The Celtics are successful because they invariably get more shots than their opponents and this can be attributed to defense—from defensive rebounding to stealing passes and causing the opponents to make errors or rush shots.

One of the greatest sights is to see five men playing an aggressive man-to-man defense; talking it up, calling switches, carrying the fight to the opposition, breaking up play patterns.

Individually, the important thing is to stay on the balls of your feet. Play flatfooted and the man you're guarding will go by you so quickly the breeze will knock you down. The knees should be bent, the back straight, head up and arms in close with the palms up.

If I'm guarding a man on the right side of the court, I have my right foot slightly forward and my right hand slightly in front of my left. I try to split my man down the middle with my front foot, which is where my weight is. If your weight is on your back foot, you lose a precious second shifting your weight to retreat.

When my man fakes to his left or right, I retreat half a step, not by crossing legs, but by shuffling back like a boxer. While retreating, I do not look at the ball, I look at my opponent's eyes. They will tell me more than any other part of his body. When you see a defensive man practically fall on the floor, you know he has gone for a head, body or leg fake.

Jump shooters usually go to their stomach or chest before firing, so by keeping your palms up, you lessen the chance of fouling him because you are coming up, not down, at the ball. Lenny Wilkins, the Hawks' all-star guard, has mastered the palms-up maneuver so well he usually steals four or five balls a game.

A jumper over Bill Russell. He's the greatest defensive player in the history of basketball.

I had to work for this one—Jim Loscutoff (18) kept me away from the basket so I went up for the jumper.

Here I get one—no pressure from the defense—a rare occurrence against Boston.

This time Russell gets one on me. Though not a great shot, through practice and concentration he has become a good scorer.

The Celtics were always tough off the boards but here I got good position on Russell and made a tip.

The 1958 championship game. This basket gave us the lead late in the game and we finally won 110-109—the game and the World Championship.

When my man shoots, I try to make it as hard as possible for him to get a good look at the basket. Anything you do to break a shooter's concentration is a tremendous help.

I almost always protect the baseline, encouraging my man to drive across the middle, where I can receive help from my guards and center. Give your man the baseline and if he gets by, he has an easy layup.

No defensive man will be able to stop the man he is guarding from taking shots, but it is the defender's job to see that his man does not take his favorite shots from his favorite spots on the floor.

A major fault on defense is waiting for the offensive man to get the ball before moving up to challenge him. The alert defender tries to force his man as far away from the basket as possible. I like to get between my man and the ball; if he wants the ball, he has to move away from the basket to get it.

Any player who does not have defensive pride is not a complete player. What good is it if you score 20 points and your opponent gets 25? Defense wins games. The Boston Celtics have been proving that for years.

Offensively, Boston has maintained the ideal blend of "sacrificers" to go along with their shooters. Setting up plays, passing, screening, feeding are arts in themselves, but they demand sacrifice as well as skill. Boston's sacrificers are also scorers, increasing their value.

The Celtics have had balanced scoring throughout the years; in fact, you'll find that the league scoring leader is usually not on a first-place club. When I won the scoring championship in 1958-59, it was the first time in eight years—since George Mikan—that the scoring leader was on a first-place team.

Here I must mention Bob Cousy because he contributed more to basketball than any other player since I have been in the game. In the years when the NBA was struggling for survival and recognition, it was George Mikan and Cousy who did most to put the game over because they were so appealing to fans—Mikan for his bulk and size and shooting prowess and Cousy for his spectacular dribbling, playmaking and passing. Bob actually made sacrificing more exciting than shooting.

Cousy gave as much to the game as he took from it. He was the most spectacular player I have ever seen. There has never been a player who could bring a crowd to its feet like he could.

I got to know Bob well during the summer of 1958 when we were both invited to participate in a new television show called "Brains and Brawn."

Actually, Bob and I competed against one another shooting different kinds of shots for money. We each had a partner in the "Brains" category. Mine was Deems Taylor and Cousy's was Alec Templeton. They would answer questions on opera and we would shoot baskets. At the end of the show, whichever team answered the most questions and made the most baskets won all the money, which was scaled according to the difficulty of the question and the shot.

Mr. Taylor and Mr. Templeton answered all of their questions so it came down to the shooting accuracy of Cooz and me. We matched one another shot for shot for three weeks. We shot free throws for $1,000; jump shots for $2,000; hook shots for $3,000 and for the grand finale, 40-foot set shots for $4,000. We were a couple of nervous fellows as we came up to our last shots, and the playing conditions didn't help any. You could hardly see the hoop for all the lights and props hanging from the studio ceiling, but I made my long set shot and Cooz missed his and Deems Taylor and I split something like $13,000. After that I never heard about the show anymore. I wonder if we broke the bank. And who knows—maybe on some old-timer's day we'll meet again in a rematch.

Chapter 13 ● I BELIEVE ● I indicated before that religion has always been a part of my life from the time I served as an altar boy at St. James Episcopal Church. Then, of course, the church helped me when I was floundering around as a teen-ager and had been cut from the high school basketball team. Playing church league ball really gave me my start.

I owe the church a lot and I have tried to repay it the best way I know how—by living an exemplary life because I know young people look up to and emulate professional athletes in all sports. During my eleven years in professional basketball, I have done only one thing for which I was ashamed. That is the only thing I would change if I had my career to live over.

It was right after my second year in the league—the year I won the scoring championship. I was in New York and a man called me and offered me an opportunity to do a cigarette commercial.

"But I don't smoke," I protested.

"It doesn't matter," the man said. "A lot of athletes endorse products they don't use."

"Yes, but it would be taking money under false pretenses," I answered. "And, besides, a lot of kids look up to me and all."

"Look," the man said, "do you want the money or not? If you don't, I'll get someone who does."

Well, the money was good, so I took the job. I knew it was wrong but I did it anyway and at first it bothered me, but then I forgot all about it until I was in camp two years later.

On the team was a rookie, from some small midwestern school. One day after practice, we were sitting in the dressing room and he reached into his pocket and pulled out a package of cigarettes.

"Hey," I said, "do you smoke?"

"Oh, yeah," he said. "When I saw your ad on TV, I said to myself if it's good enough for Bob Pettit, it's good enough for me. So I started smoking."

I felt about two inches tall and it made me realize what an influence I had on the young people in the country. I hated that television commercial more than ever, then. I wanted to erase it, but I couldn't. It's not that I am against smoking. What anybody does is his own business, but I hated that commercial mostly because it was a lie.

The basketball schedule being what it is, I had kind of drifted away from my churchgoing. Now I started to go regularly again and about a year after the cigarette incident I got a call from a friend of mine named Ron Morris. He had played basketball at Southern Methodist University and he was now a Methodist minister. He asked me if I would come to Dallas to give a talk to some young people of his church. I said I would be happy to.

Ron said he wanted me to be what he called a "witness for Christ." I didn't know what to talk about because it was the first time I had ever expressed my beliefs to a group of people. I started talking about basketball and gradually I found it easy to drift into how the church helped me find myself as a ballplayer when I was young and what it had meant to my life.

Giving this talk in front of 400 young people and telling them things you believe in, makes a better man out of you; from that day on, I tried to lead the kind of life I had talked about. As often happens when you do something for someone else, you end up benefiting yourself.

A few months after the talk in Dallas, I was asked to go to Estes Park, Colorado, to join a group of Christian athletes who had formed an organization to help young people. A man named Don McClanen had founded the group three years

before, but not until I was called to Colorado had I ever heard
of the Fellowship of Christian Athletes.

Athletes in this organization donate their time going around
the country every chance they get to speak at churches and
before young people's groups, never receiving a penny for their
efforts. Their intention is to show a correlation between athletics
and Christianity. Too often you read scandals about athletes,
but that is not the true picture of an athlete. FCA tries to paint
the true picture.

In Colorado, I met Bob Richards, the pole vaulter; Don
Moomaw, former All-America football player at UCLA and now
a Presbyterian minister; Paul Dietzel, Otto Graham, Bob Feller
and Bill Murray. Later on I met Bobby Richardson, Rafer
Johnson, Raymond Berry and Biggie Munn, all men who wil-
lingly gave of their time and energy to help young people.

Through the FCA, I became more aware of things that should
be important in a person's life and of the responsibility I, as a
professional athlete, had to young people. I came to realize
there is more to life than just those things which satisfy my own
desires. Too many athletes are interested in getting what they
can out of a sport. Not enough of them think about what they
can contribute to a sport and to their fellow man by good
example.

Some years ago, I gave a talk at Lake Geneva, Wisconsin,
and met a young man named Bill Bradley who had just graduated from high school and was attending his first FCA conference.

Several years later I was in Estes Park and I ran into Bill
Bradley there. Bill was then a senior at Princeton and the
greatest college basketball player in the country. He was giving a talk to 700 younger people. During that evening he
mentioned my talk of three years ago and how that talk had
been a great inspiration in his life.

He said he had been confused, and listening to me helped
straighten him out a little and get him back on the proper path.
This was the nicest thing that has ever been said to me or about
me and it proved to me how you can reach young people.

This responsibility does not belong only to athletes. No matter who you are there is somebody looking to you for leadership and guidance.

I am no preacher and the best way I can explain what I feel is with a little story related to basketball. I played on a team with a fellow who was big and strong and rugged. In the beginning of my career, I was getting belted around pretty good. I didn't know how to protect myself and one day this teammate came up to me and said, "Bob, I have been watching you get beat up pretty good and I have decided to do something about it. Just remember, anytime trouble starts on the court, no matter what happens or who it is, I will be behind you. I will be there to help you, so don't worry about a thing except playing basketball."

Two weeks later trouble broke out and I was standing there and some big guy was facing me, ready to tear my head off. All of a sudden two big arms reached out around him, lifted him bodily and sat him down on his bench and held him there.

It is a great feeling to know Someone is always there behind you to help you in time of trouble and this is how I feel about my church and my religion.

Whenever I am in trouble, I feel there is Somebody all-powerful waiting to help me out and pick me up if I stumble and fall. Like my teammate, but much stronger. It is a wonderful feeling and it is the best way I can describe my faith in God.

Chapter 14 ● STARS . . . IN MY EYES ● Shot for shot, the greatest all-around shooter I have ever seen is Carl Braun. There were better shooters in each of the different shots but putting them all together—two-handed set shot, one-hand jumper, one-handed set, hook, free throw—Carl was best.

The greatest two-handed long set shot belonged to Dolph Schayes but Braun was the deadliest from the middle distances. The greatest jump shooter I have seen from a guard position was Bill Sharman and from a forward position, it would be Paul Arizin and George Yardley.

Jerry West is the greatest clutch shooter and Sharman and Schayes rate as one-two from the free throw line, a completely under-rated art.

Along with rebounding I rate free throws as the most important factors in winning games. All you have to do is check the box scores to see how foul shooting affects the final result.

When I'm at the line I first get comfortable. I used to take a deep breath and let the air out slowly—then I would shoot. The deep breath has become a sort of trade-mark with me—it may or may not help you to better your game.

I shoot my free throws one-handed, my aim being to put the ball just over the front rim. I try to do this by aiming for the back part of the hoop. I follow the same rules I do on the jump shot, keeping my shoulder, elbow and hand in a direct line toward the basket. Holding the ball just below my eyes I rise on my tiptoes, flipping the ball up with a flick of the wrists and off my fingertips. I lean forward as I let fly. On the follow-through I extend my arm fully, the palm facing the floor.

If I were to learn all over again, though, I would shoot two-handed underhand free throws. A lot of people feel that you should shoot your free throws the same way you shoot your outside set shots. I just happen to feel that in the late stages of a ball game when you step up to that line, put two hands on the ball and just relax, there is a smaller margin for error shooting underhand. You have better control of the ball with two hands, a clear view of the target, and less effort is needed than with the one-handed shot. This can be an important factor late in the ball game.

As I said, I relax before shooting a free throw by taking a deep breath, then slowly let the air out of my lungs. Concentrating is simply a matter of shutting out the outside world. In this respect, my all-time favorite is Sharman. When Sharman was at the line, a bomb could go off and he wouldn't blink an eye.

Regardless of the method used for foul shooting, practice is the key to success. Dolph Schayes would inject the element of competition into practice by challenging Johnny Kerr to a shooting duel. Then Schayes would labor towards pin-point accuracy by counting his shots "made" only if the ball did not touch any part of the rim. Whether Dolph shot fifty practice shots a day or two hundred, his idea was to make every shot count.

I always shot at least fifty practice free throws a day during the season. However, in practice I didn't spend too much time at the line between shots. I don't agonize over my free throws. Relax, concentrate, and fire. I feel that anybody who works at it can learn to shoot 70 percent or better at the foul line. And anybody who learns to shoot 70 percent with added work and practice can make it 80 percent or more. The success of your foul shooting is literally in your own hands.

Along with the underhand free throws I definitely think there is a place for the two-handed set shot today. Most boys coming out of college don't work at it but it's a good long distance shot and helpful, too, for banking angle shots in close. I would have liked to use this shot when I was finishing up.

I never wanted to get burdened with too many shots, however. It's fine for a player to believe in variety but the important thing is to develop and perfect the basic shots.

In the same regard, I believe it's foolish to spend hours learning to shoot with either hand. In all my professional seasons the only player I've seen shoot equally well right and left is Dolph Schayes. This was because Dolph broke his right hand many years ago and it became necessary for him to use his left.

I've seen high school and college boys use both hands in practice but when the game is underway, they revert to the hand where the percentage is highest. So I say stay with your best hand all the time, including layups. The only exception I would make would be on the hook shot. Since the hand you use for the hook usually depends on where your defensive man is playing, it's good to be a two-way hook shooter. But I'd draw the line right there.

I give my all-time hook shooting honors to Cliff Hagan. Cliff has the best hook, left or right handed, and perfect form along with it. As for the big men, the greatest all-around shooter I've seen, including hooks, jumps and sets was Clyde Lovellette.

The hook shot is primarily the property of the pivot man, although many occasions arise when the forward is required to hook. Hagan and Lovellette represent different schools in the art of hook shoooting.

Hagan, at 6' 4", has mastered the jumping hook, which he shoots in stride with the grace of a ballet dancer. When Cliff is in the act of shooting, both his feet are approximately 12 to 15 inches off the floor. He needs this spring to compensate for his lack of height and, he has so perfected his move, it is unusual to see anyone block his hook shot.

By contrast, Lovellette, who is 6' 9" simply rises to his tiptoes when he hooks. Compared to Hagan's sweeping motion, Clyde shoots with a quick turn, but with the same deadly effect.

When I shot my hook I tried to make sure I was within reasonable range of the basket. Since the shot is begun with your

The Celtic fast break led by Bob Cousy (with ball) is probably the greatest offensive power the NBA has ever seen. Note the hustle that has four Celtics over half court with just three seconds gone on the 24-second clock.

Here's the most exciting player ever to play in the NBA, Bob Cousy, doing his specialty—committing a whole defense to him while he gets ready to pass to a teammate who is free under the basket.

The Big "O," Oscar Robertson. To my way of thinking, he's the greatest all-around player in basketball.

Elgin Baylor (22) of Los Angeles probably has the greatest offensive talent in the history of basketball. Truly an all-time great.

Here I drive under and past Wilt Chamberlain to score. Wilt will soon break my scor
record and set records that probably will never be matched.

The most valuable player in the history of the NBA has to be Bill Russell. His arrival on the scene with the Celtics took them from a very good team to the greatest team in the history of basketball and probably all sports. With Russell, the Celtics have won seven of eight World Championships —seven in a row!

Jerry West shown shooting against the Celtics is the greatest shot in basketball. He will be an all-time great before his career ends.

back to the basket, I had an idea where the hoop was only after checking the lines in the keyhole area. Assuming I have good position, I begin the hook shot with the ball at my waist, taking a step away from the basket and keeping my foot nearest the basket as the pivot.

As I turn my body, I raise my right leg and bend my right knee. I turn my head for a clear look at the basket. I emphasize this for many hook shots go astray when the shooter merely takes a quick peek at the goal. As the ball is released, my right arm is fully extended.

In shooting a right-handed hook, the left arm is invaluable as "protection." I always hold it away from my body with the elbow pointed at my defensive man, in order to keep him as far away as possible. The well-executed hook, taken with the arm fully extended and the ball rolling off the finger tips, is virtually impossible to block.

I shoot my hooks as firmly and as crisply as I can, lobbing the ball, aiming for as high a spot on the backboard as I feel will get me home. Experience has taught me the higher the bank the better. It decreases the margin of error. The only time I go for the basket and not the backboard is on hook shots when I'm directly in front of the hoop. Otherwise I try to bank them in.

It takes a real basketball craftsman to maneuver the ball into position to set up a shot. This can be done by dribbling, passing or a combination of both.

The greatest ball handlers I have ever seen are Bob Cousy and Oscar Robertson. You just couldn't get the ball away from them. They dribbled with something in mind—to set up a good play, not just to get the ball to the other end of the court.

The greatest long passer was Cousy. The greatest playmaker was Dick McGuire and if I had to pick one man I would have liked to play with it would be Dick. He, more than anyone I have seen, would have complemented my style of playing. Cousy and Oscar Robertson rate as great playmakers and Oscar gets my vote as the greatest all-around player.

I feel a man should keep his feet on the floor at all times and

never leave the floor until he is ready to make a shot. If I
jumped too soon, I would be left up in the air and would have
to make a bad shot or a poor pass. Sometimes a player will leave
the floor to make a pass and if he succeeds, it is a spectacular
play. It's always a gamble, though, and in my opinion, a poor
one.

The best defensive rebounder without a doubt is Bill Russell.
Elgin Baylor is a great offensive rebounder as are Bailey Howell
and Tom Heinsohn. Offensive rebounding is nothing but a lot
of hard work. It is just driving at that board play after play.
A lot of guys just don't want to work that hard. The best small
defensive players I would say have to be Slater Martin, K.C.
Jones and Larry Costello. Russell, of course, at center and Tom
Sanders, Mel Hutchins and Woody Sauldsberry among the forwards were the best big men on defense.

The fastest guard I have ever seen would have to be Larry
Costello, without a doubt. Frank Brian and Slater Martin were
very fast and would be ranked right with Larry.

As far as I am concerned, Elgin Baylor is one of the finest
basketball players who ever lived. I played with him in about
six or seven All-Star games and I don't think I have said ten
words to him the whole time, which is something I regret because he is an outstanding person. He certainly is a great basketball player.

We try to keep most players away from the baseline and
into the middle. But with Elgin we try to force him to the baseline where he will pull up and shoot his jump shot. If you let
him get to the middle he starts wheeling and dealing across
the circle and shooting those hook shots or drives in or passes off
to the open man. He's just too tough to stop. That's why it's
a better gamble to force him to the baseline and make him
shoot his jump shot. Whoever is playing him then has to concentrate on blocking him off the backboard.

What we tried to do on Jerry West was to play him as tight
as we could. The ones who have the best luck with Jerry are
the players who use their hands and body against him to keep
Jerry off balance as much as possible. West liked to use Rudy

La Russo as a screen. I always played La Russo so I could jump out on Jerry to help out. An automatic switch would occur. The danger was that West might hit La Russo rolling toward the basket for a layup. But we always gambled that Jerry was looking more for the basket than to pass. There is no way you can stop West because he has so many great offensive moves. He gets the shot off too quickly to block it. Our play was to make him hurry his shots and to force him to shoot outside his high percentage area.

Sam Jones is such a complete ball player we try to do the same thing with him. The basic thing we try to do is switch, and just jump out on him as soon as he goes behind a pick.

You pray on Oscar. There is very little else you can do. Jack Twyman we played tight and never sloughed off him because he doesn't drive much.

Paul Arizin we tried to force to the baseline and played him tight. Cousy we played tight and forced him to drive because he had a good outside shot. You never steal the ball from him. You just play your position between Cooz and the basket and keep the pressure on him but give with him. Try to keep him taking that one-handed shot so your back man could pick him up.

Richie Guerin is as good a driver as I have ever seen. Baylor has the best body control.

If I were to choose one played to build a winning team around it would be Bill Russell. He gets my Most Valuable Player selection. If I were to choose one player with the most talent—taking in all phases of the game—it would be Oscar Robertson.

The game has changed drastically from my rookie year in 1954 to my last year, 1965. Mikan was great in his era and with the team with which he was associated, but the style of play has changed so much that even Mikan would have to make many adjustments in his play if he were able to come back today.

While we are in that vein, I have also been asked many times to compare the players who were around in my rookie year with those who were in the league when I played my last game. I don't think there is any comparison. The players of today are the greatest who have ever played the game and the players ten years from now will be greater than those playing right now and so on.

Everything in life is improved, why not basketball? The players are bigger, stronger, better coached, jump higher, shoot better and run faster. In any sport which is measured by time and distance—for example, swimming, track and field—the records keep getting better. So it is safe to assume basketball players are improving just as swimmers and track men and they are better now than they have ever been.

If you want to check some basketball figures, though, take a peek at the heights and weights of the first NBA players in 1946-47 and compare them with the vital statistics of the players of today.

Then look at the shooting percentages of the teams that first year in the league and compare them with the percentages made in my last season, 1964-65.

In the league's first year, no team was able to make thirty percent of its shots from the floor. In my last year of play, every team was over forty percent. And they're still improving.

Chapter 15 ● REFLECTIONS . . . REMEMBRANCES . . . RECOMMENDATIONS ● When you're running, shooting, and passing during a ball game, the moves are quick, almost automatic. You see an opening and react. There's no time for deliberation.

By contrast, shooting free throws, particularly in a clutch situation, can be a time of great tension. Standing still with time to think, you become increasingly conscious of what the situation means.

In fact, the opposition coach may call a timeout before a particularly important foul shot, feeling that the added time may make the shooter even more nervous before he steps up to the line.

My most dramatic experience at the foul line was in Los Angeles in my final year. We were one point down. The buzzer went off when I was in the act of shooting and I was fouled by Leroy Ellis. I had two free throws. I had to make one to tie the game, two to win it. There were about 12,000 people in Los Angeles screaming at me as I went up to the line. A lot of things go through your mind.

In this particular instance I said two things to myself, "All right, big man, you think you are so tough and so good, then just show me something. This is your big chance." And the second thing I said was, "*Just* make the first one." Fortunately, I made them both and we won the game.

It would be satisfying to reflect that it always happened like this, but such was not the case. Sometimes I blew an important shot, despite bearing down. You feel awfully bad inside, but I tried not to brood about it once I left the arena. I welcomed shooting in a tight situation. If we were two points down, I would always want the ball. I always had the confidence I could make it.

During a game there are many things to keep in mind. It is most important at all times to know how much time is left. A lot of maneuvering is based on personal fouls and team fouls. The number of timeouts left can be a factor.

I always was aware of the strengths and weaknesses of the man I was playing against, as well as his method of playing me.

For example, when we played in Boston, Tom Sanders was matched against me. He liked to play between the guard and me when the ball was coming down my side of the court. What I would try to do is run a baseline play, where our guard takes the ball like he is going to the other side of the court, dribbles, and comes back to me on an angle. I take one step like I'm going behind him, then I go baseline and he bounces the ball to me for a layup.

Even if my man recovered to stop my guard from making the pass, he realized I was able to go baseline on him and he could no longer play in front of me. I would always do this during the first part of the game. After that, I was able to go behind and use my guard as a screen.

If I were playing defense and guarding Tom Heinsohn, although he's a fine outside shooter, I still want to get him as far away from the basket as possible. I want him to take his shots from the top of the foul circle instead of the foul line. I always tried to force him to the middle because he is a great baseline driver. To do this, I overplayed him into the middle, trying to keep him away from the baseline and into a position when I could get help from the guards. Once he got into the middle I would try to force him as far away from the basket as I could before he took his shot.

Just as players have their individual ways of doing things,

so do officials. It helps to learn from experience what each will call and what he lets go.

I guessed wrong on an official's reaction in an important game that Sid Borgia was handling in Detroit. It was the only game I was thrown out of in my entire career, and it happened in the final regular game of the 1964-65 season.

We were one game behind San Francisco in the standings and we were 17 points down to the Pistons in the third quarter. At the beginning of the last quarter we began making our move. We cut the lead to nine.

Mike Farmer had the ball at our end of the court and he went up for a layup and was fouled in the act of shooting, I thought. But Borgia called it a one-shot play and I went to him and said, "Sid, I think you blew that call. I think it was a two pointer."

Sid said, "Well, Bob, you're right. I did miss it."

I didn't say anything. What could I say? We went to the other end of the court and I got the ball on the defensive rebound and got knocked to the floor. I threw the ball to Wilkins and he got slammed to the side by a Detroit player, who picked up the ball and scored.

I really jumped at Sid and hollered at him. I am not proud of what I did and certainly deserved a technical foul, but I never thought that Sid would throw me out of the game— certainly not a game that meant so much. Our team lost. If I had been in, I think we might have won because I had 29 points at that stage with 10 minutes left, and I was hitting. My early shower could have cost us the Western Division championship because if we had won that game and San Francisco lost we would have played them one game in a playoff for the title.

Basketball is probably the toughest game in the world to officiate. With ten big men crammed into a small area and the present speed of the game, the officials are under constant pressure to make quick, accurate calls.

Across the country, you'll find that even the most competent officials differ in their interpretations of the foul rules. Gradually more of a standardization is taking place, but many college scouting reports still tip teams off as to how they should play to stay within the rules when they play a rival from a different section of the country. Maybe some day through a national officials' school or through films or books there will be some way to create a uniformity of interpretation by all officials.

One of my pet peeves in my last few years of play was the offensive foul. No free throw results, but the foul is charged against the player and his team loses the ball. A good official usually calls this right, but too often the poor official makes this his "when in doubt" call.

It's difficult to single out one official and say that he was the finest of a good group. I do have a choice, though. He's Mendy Rudolph.

I found Mendy an informed official who kept calm and cool and never argued with the players. He made his calls decisively, but was not hasty. He had full control of the game at all times.

In any sport, there is room for improvement, and basketball is no exception. I would hope that some day all the teams draw enough fans and get enough television revenue so that the schedule can be shortened and the wear and tear on the players can be reduced.

I'd like to see a long shot beyond an established line become a three pointer. It would stand out like a home run in baseball. It also might take some of the premium away from the dunk shot, which I believe hurts the game. Fans get tired of seeing the ball get dunked night after night.

I very seldom dunked the ball. I always felt the shot was designed more for show than effectiveness. I used it only when I went up for a shot in an awkward position, and couldn't lay my shot up correctly because I was off balance.

I always thought I had a better chance at making my shot off the backboard. Too often I have seen guys attempt to dunk and miss, either by ramming their hand or the ball against the rim. Also, with a dunk, because you have to leave your feet and go high up in the air, there's an increased risk of injury. For all these reasons, I rarely dunked the ball.

Chapter 16 ● UP FOR THE GAME ● You hear a lot of guys say they can't get up for every game because they play so many. I agree to a point. The excitement of an important game always provided its own stimulation for me, but for some of the routine games where there was little at stake, I worked to provide my own psychological inducements.

I wanted every game to be the big game for me and to insure this feeling if it weren't naturally there, I'd work at finding some extra incentive to goad myself into increased effort. Whether it was a contrived reason or a valid one, by the time I took the court, I knew that nothing but my best performance would suffice. I had to win.

You may laugh at some of the ways I psyched myself into getting up for games—I do in retrospect—but they all served their purpose at the time.

I remember one game in St. Louis. It was near the end of the season, the result had no bearing on the standings, and I was thinking ahead to the playoffs. Yet the fans were expecting to see a heated battle and maybe a few of them had come out to see me in action. I kept searching for a reason to work myself up for the game.

On the way to the locker room, I happened to look at the crowd and my attention was drawn to an attractive girl near courtside. I had never seen her before and I don't recall ever seeing her again, but somehow I felt determined to win her applause. I was going to make her sit up and take notice. When the game started, I concentrated on the play so much

145

I don't know what her reaction was, but I do remember that I went into the game with an extra incentive and I'm sure it made a difference in my play.

I never lacked for a reason. Maybe the game was to be televised. I would think of the youngsters who might be looking at me for the first time, watching me as an example for their own play. I had to be at my best.

Sometimes I knew my family would be watching on television. Maybe coaches, ball players or close friends who had seen me during the years would be watching also. They knew the way I worked. They'd be observing closely. I'd want to prove that I was still going forward, not backward.

In some cities, New York, for example, getting up for a game was easier. In Madison Square Garden, the setting, the atmosphere, the battery of reporters, seemed to give each game added importance. And, of course in St. Louis, where fans and writers and radio-TV reporters were so good to me during the years, I felt I owed them a special effort.

Above all else, though, were two inner forces which kept me bearing down. One was pride in giving my best. I viewed each game as a new test. There was no resting on the past. I had to prove myself again. I might win or I might lose, but I wanted to come out of every game knowing in my heart that I had given the best that was in me.

The other motivating force was a sense of obligation to so many people. My coach, my teammates were counting on me to be at my peak. All those who rooted for me, all those who had worked with me, I carried all their hopes into action. And at every game were those who paid to see me, whether they were for our team or against it. The obligation was always there.

When I got through with a game, I didn't need a statistics sheet to tell me how I played. I knew inside. There have been nights when I scored well, but I was also aware of mistakes I had made. Many things can go wrong in a ball game which don't show up in the box scores—poor passes, slow reaction, bad positioning, mental mistakes—the list is endless.

There were other games, when I may not have scored well, but I was pleased with my play. I made the right moves to help my team win.

Ball players can contribute in many ways. Some spark a club with hustle and spirit. They keep the team alive. They keep moving, stay alert, bear down on defense. On the sidelines, they shout encouragement. They're team players.

I've also seen the other type come and go. Players who may have good ability but poor attitude. This can show in many ways. They may loaf at times, put out when they're winning but not when they're losing. They may act uninterested if they're not playing regularly, they may be on the team but not really a part of it. These are the also-rans, not the champions.

Being mentally up for a game insures giving a top effort, but despite this, sometimes, things don't go well. If I were having a poor game, I'd try to compensate with increased physical exertion in my rebounding. Often I would get frantic and rip and tear and claw to get to the offensive backboard, because when I was missing my shots, my scoring came off the offensive backboards. I would find that on my bad nights, I was a better offensive rebounder than on the nights when I was getting my jumper.

When your jumper isn't working, you have to concentrate to get your points on the offensive boards. When I would come out for the second half, I would talk to myself. "All right, Pettit, you stunk the first half. Now go out there and show these people something the second half. These people came out to see you play and they think you are going to be good, so let's show them something."

I would concentrate on my shooting. I liked to come out early at half time and take a lot of jump shots. When I was missing, there were always two or three things wrong—I was falling away from the basket or I was holding the ball too long before I released it or I was falling from side to side or I wasn't going into the basket enough. I would try to see what was wrong and get back in the groove at half time.

Anytime I missed my first six or eight shots, I didn't panic and start forcing. I was confident if I missed my first six shots, I was going to make my next six. Sometime during the ball game I would have a streak where I would start hitting.

I knew at every minute how many points I had. Not that I made an effort to keep track of them, but for some reason they just clicked in my mind. And usually I would know how many points the man I was playing had.

I rarely replayed a game after it was over unless I had a particularly bad night or a particularly good one. If I scored 55 points I would be very happy for a couple of hours afterwards, but by the next day I had forgotten about it. I began thinking of the next game.

The clutch games were ones in which I needed no additional inner urging. The fire inside me was all stoked up and burning brightly in advance. I couldn't wait, and I always had the feeling that nothing could stop me. When the chips were down, I wanted to be in on it. I wanted the ball when it counted. I knew I had the power within me to win.

The better I did, the hungrier I got for more. There was always a new height to attain, and I didn't want to stop. Confidence can be a mighty weapon.

Another priceless ingredient is enthusiasm. Enthusiasm puts the fun in work. I like enthusiasm on the bench, on the court and in the stands. People speak about the home-court advantage. I don't believe that it's a physical difference—to me it's psychological, the enthusiasm of home-town fans. The inspiration may mean six or eight points a ball game, cheering for baskets, imploring you to come from behind if you trail.

Enthusiasm also helps to gather new fans for the sport. I remember how important broadcaster Buddy Blattner was in our growing years in St. Louis with his lively accounts of our ball games. He conveyed the excitement of the sport to new fans in the area. It was Buddy, incidentally, who hung the tag "Big Blue" on me during his broadcasts because of an old blue overcoat that I wore at the time. The coat has long since been put away, but with many people the nickname still remains.

The ball player has to realize that he is in the public spotlight at all times. His conduct, what he says and does, makes news. This imposes a great need for self-control.

I hate to see a player make gestures or argue with people in the stands. Letting the fans sound off is part of the game.

All athletes—particularly star athletes—have the power to influence others for good—or for bad.

There are thousand of youngsters throughout the country who identify their budding careers with established stars. When an athlete who has been admired reveals himself as boastful or unsportsmanlike or deceitful—or if he is dishonest or immoral or lacking in good judgment in any way—he not only hurts himself, but far worse, he is destroying all that has been built up in his young followers—in fact, some may even follow down the wrong path.

Controversy, unfortunately, makes more headlines than good deeds. I deplore the selfishness of those who have excelled as athletes—and yet have let down so many by failing to measure up as people.

Not that resisting the temptations that befall an athlete is easy. Who can say that he never made a mistake. The glory, the fame—in some cases, the fortune—make the athlete an open target for all sorts of people with designs, particularly in travels on the road. It's a cinch to find someone to lead you down the wrong path. It takes a little guts, though, to resist the temptations that exist. The athlete not only has to face his own conscience, but has to realize that in any transgression he's hurting his family, his friends and those young fellows on the way up who believe in him.

And if all this won't keep the athlete on the right path, remember this. It's also good business not to risk destroying a whole career because of an off-the-court mistake.

Just as one works for years to become a top athlete, one should work to develop an image as a person—a pattern of conduct—standards by which one is known and respected. This is a goal towards which you dedicate yourself in everything you do and say.

Scoring records as a basketball player are a matter of great personal pride, but your record as a person is the most important record of all.

Chapter 17 ● DECISION ● I can't exactly pinpoint when I made my decision to retire or what was the deciding factor. There were many things—the weariness of travel, the irregularity of the life, the aches and pains and broken bones which seemed to be coming more frequently as the years passed.

Maybe Mr. Clifford Ourso had a good deal to do with my decision. He is the President and Chairman of the Board of the American Bank and Trust Company in Baton Rouge and in the fall of 1962 he requested a meeting with me. He offered me a very good position with the bank and for the first time in my life, I had an offer which really appealed to me, so much, I began thinking of retiring from basketball.

At last I had the opportunity to go into a business which I would be happy to make my life's work. I played that year and worked in the bank during the off season and that was all I needed to convince me I would be making the right decision. I always loved business and financing and, of course, all business comes through a banker's desk.

Well, that had a good deal to do with my retirement—at least thinking of retiring. First, there was some unfinished business still to be accomplished in the National Basketball Association.

Before the 1963-64 season, I went to Mr. Kerner and told him of my decision. I would play one more year, two at most, and then go into the bank. During that season, I broke Dolph Schayes' all-time scoring record and when the season ended, I had 19,756 points. That was one record I wanted badly and it was the main reason I played the season, although I am

glad I played for another reason, which has nothing to do with
points, rebounds or championships.

In January of 1964, there was a development that is vital
to every player in the NBA and everyone who ever will play
basketball in the NBA and I am proud to have been a part of
such a thing.

About six or seven years before, Bob Cousy had been instrumental in forming a Players' Association, whose main objective was a pension plan and player recognition. The owners
were reluctant to give us a pension fund but in 1962 it was
agreed at a meeting in New York between owners and players
that we would start a pension plan. It had never gone into
effect, even though it had been agreed upon. Bob Cousy had
retired as Chairman of the Players' Association, Tom Heinsohn
had replaced him and I was Vice-President. It was agreed that
the All-Star game in Boston in January 1964, was the time for
the owners and players to put the plan into practice.

The All-Stars felt they were the ones who should get it
started. I had already decided this was my next to last year so
I had nothing to gain because it isn't retroactive. But we all
felt we had to get it sometime and this was the time.

I left St. Louis on a Monday morning and went to the airport, but I was snowed in, so I took the train. The All-Star
game was in Boston at 9 o'clock on Tuesday night and I didn't
get to Boston until four that afternoon.

I walked into the Sheraton-Plaza Hotel and about three
players came running up to me and said, "We are having a
meeting in the room. The owners wouldn't see us." I didn't
really know what had happened. So I went up to the room
and every player on the All-Stars was there. At noon they went
to speak to the owners and were not able to get in to see them.
The players were very upset and someone suggested if they
wouldn't give us our pension plan, we wouldn't play the All-
Star game.

There was much arguing back and forth. During this time
I really got to know and have admiration for Tommy Heinsohn.
He has as much intestinal fortitude as any man I have ever

Receiving my second Most Valuable Player award. This one was for the 1959 season and it was awarded at the 1960 All Star game by then Commissioner Podoloff.

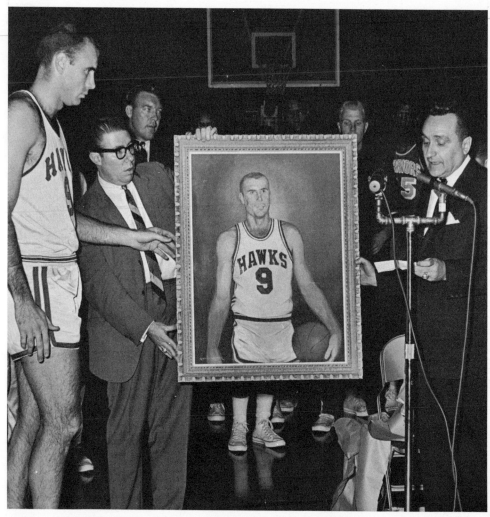

Bob Pettit Night and Mr. Ben Kerner presented me with a portrait of myself.

The shot that broke the 20,000 point barrier.

Ouch! This is the play that broke several bones in my back. I was out for 4 weeks. And they call this a non-contact sport!

Cincinnati Royal President Carl Rich presents me with a cake and Mr. Kerner assists. They stopped the game for this, my biggest moment in basketball.

Mr. Kerner couldn't continue with his speech at the press conference where I announced my decision to retire after the 1964-65 season.

It hurt greatly to make that announcement and I dreaded doing so. My face reflects my feelings.

known and I think he really showed it this day. He was not necessarily in favor of striking, but he was President of the Association. "Look, fellows, this is Boston and it is my hometown but if you feel the only way we can get a pension plan is to strike and not play the game tonight, don't let this bother you. You just go ahead and do whatever you want. Whatever you vote for I will go along with."

We had several alternatives. I suggested we wait until the owners' meeting in the spring and tell them we wanted our pension plan or else we wouldn't sign our contracts for the next year.

I didn't like the idea of waiting till the last minute to call off the game but the players voted not to play the All-Star game unless we got our pension. They also selected two men to go see Walter Kennedy, the new Commissioner of the NBA, and the two men chosen were Tom Heinsohn and Bob Pettit, as President and Vice-President of the Association. This happened about 5:00 p.m.

I will never forget Bob Pettit and Tom Heinsohn walking around the Sheraton-Plaza Hotel. I think these were the two most scared men in New England because we would bear the brunt of the criticism if the game were not played.

At 6:15, Tom and I went to see Mr. J. Walter Kennedy, whom I did not know very well because it was his first year as Commissioner. We knocked on his door and he answered, wearing a dressing gown.

"Fellows," he said, "I have a dinner appointment, can I see you later?"

"Well, sir," I said, "it's about the pension plan."

"Can we talk about it tomorrow?"

"I'm afraid not," Tommy said. "We have to talk about it right now."

"Does it have anything to do with tonight's game?"

"Yes," Tom said, "it does."

So, Mr. Kennedy invited us in and asked us to sit down and Tom said, "It has been the vote of the players that unless we get the pension plan in writing now, we are not going to play the game tonight. We feel we have been put off long enough."

Mr. Kennedy thought a while, then calmly said, "Fellows, I can't give you an answer now. Some of the owners are not here, but I will meet you in your dressing room tonight at 8:30 and do what I can." Since the game was scheduled to start at 9:00, I figured he was cutting it pretty thin.

We went to the arena and got dressed and were just sitting around and at 8:30 in walked Commissioner Kennedy with Haskell Cohen, the league publicity director. Haskell kept saying, "You can't do this, you can't do this."

But the Commissioner kept his composure and I really had to admire him even though we were on opposite sides in the bargaining. He was really on the spot, it being his first year and all and he was kind of in the middle.

"Fellows," he said, "I'm not going to give you the plan in writing. I can't let you pin my back to the wall this way, but I'll tell you what I'll do. I'll give you my word that I will do everything in my power to see that you get your pension plan.

"I want you to realize what you're doing. If you don't play this game tonight, you will ruin pro basketball. You'll ruin it here in Boston and you'll ruin it across the country. You know this game is being televised tonight. If it doesn't go on, you'll destroy any chances we have of staying on national television.

"You have my word that I'll do everything I can to help you. That is all I can do and it is up to you to make your decision."

It was about five minutes to nine and Haskell Cohen was just about to have a kitten right there in the dressing room. They left the room. Some of the players wanted to play and others didn't. I personally felt we had to go out there and play that game. We had made our point and we would only be hurting ourselves if we didn't play.

Wilt Chamberlain stood up and said, "Look, fellows, we have no choice. We have to play this game so let's go."

I was proud of Wilt. Then we put it to a vote and the decision was to play. We walked out on the court at about one minute to nine and went on TV at nine. At the next owners' meeting in New York Mr. Kennedy did just what he promised and the pension plan was put into effect.

It pleased me to know I had had even a small part in helping to put the pension fund over. It is one of the things I am happy to have been associated with, kind of my personal and private legacy to the sport which did so much for me.

I had accomplished almost everything I wanted to accomplish when the 1963-64 season ended. I had broken Dolph Schayes' record for most points in a career. I knew that record would not last the way Wilt is scoring points, but still I wanted to do it.

Now there was one other thing I wanted to accomplish and that convinced me to come back for the 1964-65 season. When I made it, this would be one thing they could never take away from me. I needed only 244 points to become the first player in the history of the game to score 20,000 points and I knew I had to do this because there is only one "first."

When I retired, I was to be put in charge of all business and industrial development in the American Bank and be given the title of Vice-President. My mind was practically made up. My family had been begging me to retire and I remember, in particular, my mother's brother, Dr. John Brandon, sitting down with me one evening. He was my greatest fan and he once said he would hate the day I quit professional basketball, but he was a practical man and this night he said, "Bob, I think it is time for you to get out."

I went to camp that summer and told Mr. Kerner I had definitely made up my mind the 1964-65 season would be my last. Nothing could change that. I explained that after I had passed the 20,000-point plateau, there would be nothing left for me in the game. I would have had all the personal and team honors I possibly could win.

The funny thing is I felt I could play perhaps two more years and still maintain an average of 20 points a game, but I didn't want to continue like that. I could feel the spring going from my legs and realized everything, from then on, would be downhill and I wanted to retire while I was on top. I would be playing below the standards I set for myself and one thing I never wanted to do was play below my own standards.

Mr. Kerner understood. He couldn't have been kinder about it when I told him of my plans as I was signing my last pro basketball contract. I knew he wouldn't try to talk me out of it, but he said, "I don't think you will gain anything by announcing your retirement before the season. I think it would be more to your advantage to announce it after the All-Star game in St. Louis."

I agreed to do it that way.

I started the season and in a way, it was the must frustrating season I have ever experienced. The club did not go well, mainly because we were hit with more injuries that year than I have ever seen. I was injured three times and missed about eight weeks of the season. The injuries had nothing to do with my retirement because I had already made up my mind. But if I hadn't, they would have convinced me to get out.

My big night came in Cincinnati on November 13. Friday the 13th and it is a good thing I wasn't superstitious. I needed seven points to make 20,000 and I remember it was in the second quarter and I had six points. I was conscious of how close I was to becoming the first player to go over 20,000 points and I realized I needed just one more field goal.

I missed two or three shots and then one of my teammates took a shot and it missed and bounced high in the air. Jerry Lucas was defending me and the ball bounced over his hands and I went up and got it about seven feet from the hoop. I came down, then went up again and tossed a jump-hook shot —something I had picked up from Billy McGill just that year —it went in and I had 20,001 points.

They stopped the game and Mr. Kerner presented me with the ball and Carl Rich, owner of the Royals, wheeled out a big cake and presented it to me. I was thrilled. There were a few speeches—right in the middle of the game—and they asked me to say a few words.

"This was something I really wanted," I remember saying. "Although there will be others to score 20,000 points, I'm proud as I can be that I was the first."

We lost the game, but it seemed like we had won because after it was over, reporters and photographers streamed into our dressing room. They interviewed me and many of my teammates and they took pictures of me and in the papers the next day—even in Cincinnati—there was more written about me than the Royals' victory.

I finished the game with 29 points, which gave me 20,022 for my career and it was ironic that I should break the record against a team coached by Jack McMahon. We had played together for four years and I guess Jack was responsible for me getting a couple of thousand of those points.

There was one other reason I wanted to retire and I saved it for last, not because it was unimportant, but because it is the most important reason. The story actually dates back to our world championship of 1958. When we won, Mr. Kerner vowed he would promote a night for all five of the starting players on that team. Each player had his night and mine was scheduled for March 2, 1962.

It was a night I will never forget. I received about $15,000 worth of gifts, which included a new automobile, clothes, a color television set and a trip to Hawaii.

Two close friends of mine from St. Louis, Bob and Jean Shoenberg, happened to be going to Hawaii that June, so I decided I would go with them and we would all stay at the Royal Hawaiian Hotel. I was sitting on the beach one day and a group of familiar people were walking toward me. They were Frank Gifford, Ken Venturi, Bob Cousy and Paul Hornung and they were there on a business promotion. We spent a lot of time together, playing volleyball and golf.

One day I was standing on the beach and this man walked up to me and said, "You're Bob Pettit, aren't you?"

"Yes, sir, I am."

"My name is Richard Crowell. I'm here from Alexandria, Louisiana. I'm here with my family. I just wanted to say hello."

We chatted for a few minutes and I found him to be a very warm, friendly person. He was a lawyer back home and after awhile, he invited me over to meet his family.

"Bob Pettit," he said, "I would like you to meet Mrs. Crowell. And this is my son, Richard, and my daughter Nancy and my other daughter, Carole. . . ."

Carole and I were married on June 19, 1965. We spent our honeymoon in Hawaii.

**Chapter 18 ● NOT THE END . . . ONLY THE BEGIN-
NING ●** I kept my promise and returned for the 1964-65 season and I am almost sorry I did. Except for going over the
20,000-point mark, there is little about the season I would like
to remember.

I was injured three times. I tore a muscle in my lower abdo-
men and had a lot of internal hemorrhaging. Instead of sitting
down and resting it, I continued to play and finally, I had to
sit out for two weeks.

A month later I had a collision with Rudy La Russo of the
Lakers and broke four little bones in my back, which kept me
out another month. I came back and was getting in good shape
when I tore a ligament in my left knee.

Even with all our injuries, we still managed to finish second
in our division. Then came the playoffs and we were eliminated
by Baltimore.

If that final game in Baltimore was the most frustrating day
of my professional career, it was not the saddest. That came
more than a month earlier and it was a day I had been dread-
ing all season. It came, finally, on March 1 and I would much
rather play the Celtics in the final game of the playoffs or
stand at the foul line with two shots and trailing by two points
with one second left than go through this day again.

Mr. Kerner called a press conference at Ruggeri's Restaurant in St. Louis. The place was jammed with newspapermen,
radio and television people and cameras. It was the saddest
day of my life and I would have given anything not to have

had to face it, but I always knew, sooner or later, this day would come.

Mr. Kerner had prepared a speech and he called for everyone's attention and began reading the two-page speech. He was almost halfway through when his voice started to crack and tears began streaming down his cheeks and I had to turn away and fight as hard as I could to keep from joining him.

Finally, Mr. Kerner could not continue reading his speech and he sat down and Mike Aubuchon, who is the club's attorney, had to finish it. I have a copy of that speech and I will always treasure it because it is a beautiful speech and knowing Mr. Kerner, I know it is a sincere speech. Here is what he said:

"Bob Pettit is retiring and I know that I should find solace in his records and accomplishments that remain. But I cannot. His records convey the great player but not the wonderful man.

"I know I could talk for hours about my eleven years of association with Bob—about his tremendous contributions to our success—the formation of what we call the Hawks' image; his formidable leadership in bringing us five Western Division titles and a world championship; his contributions to pro basketball and his many records.

"There isn't much I can say that hasn't already been said about his basketball ability. These accomplishments are permanently engraved in our record books.

"But I want to relate my personal feelings about Bob Pettit as I know him. Bob, by his conduct both on and off the court, has been a credit to pro basketball. He typifies the type of individual we seek in our game, not only because of his greatness on the court but because of his humility, his conscientious adaptation to his work and his great desire to excel. He has created a symbol for other Hawk players to follow and for all future pro basketball players to live up to.

"The admiration and respect that his teammates and the opposing players hold for Bob is a true indication of the stature that he commands. Perhaps Bill Russell best explained the feelings of the other players several years ago when he said, 'There's no greater competitor in sports. He's a winning ball player who made the expression, second effort, a part of the sports vocabulary.'

"Bob's best performances have always been under pressure. He's been tougher in the second half of a big game than in the first; tougher in the fourth quarter than in the third and toughest of all in the closing minutes of a game when a clutch basket might be needed.

"His greatest season—his greatest contribution—was in 1961-62 when a multitude of circumstances found us having a bad year. He never stopped hustling, never faltered one iota when you might expect a player to take it easy since obviously the cause was a futile one. Yet, Bob came through with a magnificent year, battling as only he can, to give our club some semblance of respectability and competitiveness.

"There have been and will be greater individual players but never one with more heart and dedication. His drive, his enthusiasm for the game, his tremendous desire to excel—all these qualities long ago stamped him as one of the greatest athletes of all time—a pro's pro, an owner's dream.

"My association with Bob has been more than the usual owner-player relationship.

"This is my nineteenth year in pro basketball. For the first nine years in my ever-changing search for a winning ball club and an inspirational player to lead it, the result was always the same. Maybe tomorrow—only tomorrow never came. Then I drafted Bob Pettit and everything changed. The next eleven years saw everything I had believed in and hope for come true. Bob was instrumental in making this possible.

"We must lament his retirement—you expect it eventually but you are not acclimated to accepting it when that moment finally comes. But we must be grateful for all of the thrills and excitement that he brought us in those eleven wonderful years that he was a member of the Hawks. It is a cliche to suggest that we are better for having known him but in Bob's case, the cliches are fitting and true. No individual has ever meant more to me before; no one man ever meant so much. All of us—the fans, the players, you writers, radio and TV men —will miss him. A little bit of our life will slip away when Bob leaves.

"Bob, thanks for everything."

When Mr. Kerner finished, I was called upon to speak. I had planned to say something like, "This was the most difficult decision I ever had to make," because it was. I wanted to point out how I always set high standards for myself and when I no longer felt I was able to meet those standards, I knew that would be the end. Then I wanted to mention the opportunity with the bank and how anxious I was to get started on a new career. These are the things I wanted to say and when I got up to talk the room was spinning and I was in kind of a daze and I can only hope I got across what I was trying to say.

After that, there was a question and answer session, which was much easier, but I still wanted to get away from there and be by myself. I couldn't wait until I could play again and forget all about this day.

From then on, everywhere we played I was greeted with cheers and dozens of newspapermen interviewed me and wrote stories about me. In some cities, I was presented with gifts and in St. Louis, they gave me a big night during half-time of my last regular season game.

At this final send-off there were presents and many dignitaries there and the fans gave me two standing ovations which thrilled me more than words can express.

Then someone read a telegram. It said:

> I am pleased to join Senator Symington as well as your many friends in the sports world in this tribute to you. Long after your scoring records have been forgotten, you will be remembered for your contribution to the integrity of professional sports and for your concern for the welfare of our youth. You have my warm congratulations and best wishes.
>
> *Lyndon B. Johnson*

Pleasant memories are nice to have at a career's end, but, when you're still competing, the game you're in is an all-consuming physical and emotional experience. You don't think of yesterday.

The Baltimore Civil Center scoreboard showed that my final game was over but inside of me, it was still going on. I was raging inwardly as I returned to the Hawks' locker room, aching with the agony of defeat, tormented by the frustration of sitting idly by as the last clutch minutes ticked away.

"If they had just given me the ball—given me the chance—just let me go out giving all I had . . ." The thought kept pounding within me. I looked down at my injured leg and tried to understand.

There had been defeats before, but always the chance to come back the next day, or the next trip, or even the next year to rub out the pain of losing. Always the chance to drive yourself harder and harder; to somehow find that extra force within you—to never let up until you win. But now . . .

I showered and began to dress, trying to compose myself. My teammates came over to say their good-byes. The room began to empty. I looked up and saw that Bailey Howell of the Baltimore Bullets was walking towards me. "Bob," he said, as he extended his hand to shake mine, "I couldn't let you leave without telling you something. I sincerely want you to know that you're the finest competitor I've ever played with or against. There's winning and losing in every game, but when I think of a winning ballplayer, I think of you. Congratulations Bob, on a great career." Bailey left, and I hoped that my words to him expressed my gratitude, not only for his comments, but for his thoughtfulness in coming by.

Strange, I thought, how the last game was so much like the beginning. At the start, I was an awkward youngster on the sidelines just hoping for a chance to play. Now at the end of my career I was on the sidelines again feeling the same frustration—the some powerful emotion inside. From the first game to the last, the drive within me had never changed. And now, as my playing career ended, I finally understood. This

drive—this desire—this had been my constant ally; this had
been the key to success. Here was something to hold on to,
something to take with me as I embarked on a new career.

My last game was over, but as I left the building, I understood . . . and was grateful.